AYYAPPA PANIKER
THE MAN BEYOND THE LITTERATEUR

AYYAPPA PANIKER
THE MAN BEYOND THE LITTERATEUR

PRIYADAS G. MANGALATH

TRANSLATED BY **RADHIKA P. MENON**

Konark Publishers Pvt. Ltd
206, First Floor,
Peacock Lane, Shahpur Jat,
New Delhi 110 049
+91-11-4105 5065
india@konarkpublishers.com, us@konarkpublishers.com
www.konarkpublishers.com

Copyright © Priyadas G. Mangalath, 2024

All rights reserved. No part of this book may be reproduced or utilised in any form or by any means, electronic or mechanical, including photocopying, recording, or by any information storage and retrieval system, without prior written permission from the author or the publisher. The views and opinions expressed in this book are solely those of the author. While the accuracy of the facts, as reported by the author, has been verified to the fullest extent possible, the publisher is not liable in any way for the content.

ISBN: 978-81-973432-6-1

Edited by Dipali Singh

Jacket design by Sourish Mitra

Cover Image © Priyadas G. Mangalath

Typeset by K.K. Gusain

Printed and bound at Saurabh Printers Pvt Ltd, Greater Noida

I closely observed his last facial expression, following his death. I did not understand anything. Not many understood this genius when he was alive. That includes me too. Even if we string together all our experiences, we will not be able to complete our study of him.

T.N. Gopakumar's Reminiscence of Ayyappa Paniker

Contents

Introduction	*ix*
Preface	*xvii*
Acknowledgements	*xxi*
1. Union Christian College	1
2. The Institute of English	7
3. The Time of Transition	12
4. John Abraham	20
5. "A Person Unknown to Me"	25
6. Prize Money	29
7. One Hundred Per Cent	34
8. *Lankesh Patrike*	39
9. More than an Artist	43
10. Modernism is Dead. Long Live Modernism	47
11. Strange Tastes	51
12. Enemy/Friend	56
13. Invisible Power	64
14. Humour in Conversation	68
15. Humour in Poetry	75
16. Humour in Prose	81

17.	As a Vibrant Presence	87
18.	Outlook on Life	98
19.	Wake-up Calls in the Field of Painting	103
20.	World Malayali	107
21.	A Gentle Presence	114
22.	Guild Soft	120
23.	A Self-Respecting Individual	123
24.	Salman Rushdie	127
25.	Who is This Man?	131
26.	The Prompter, Promoter and Witness	137
27.	*Pinnem Chankaran*	146
28.	The Iconoclastic Model	151
29.	Seeing One's Pupil as a Teacher	156
30.	Personal Profiles	159
31.	Interiorisation	164
32.	The Solitary Tree	168
33.	Awesome Paniker	173
34.	Ayyappa Paniker's Politics	178
35.	The Leading Light	184
36.	"Ayyappa Paniker is Not Profitable at all"	188
37.	Poetry at Midnight	194
38.	Variety and Contradictions	202
39.	Self-Masquerades	209
40.	Writing the Self	216
41.	Conclusion	227

Index 233

About the Author 241

About the Translator 242

Introduction

A STATEMENT WRITTEN by T.N. Gopakumar, who was the news editor-in-chief of *Asianet News,* about Ayyappa Paniker forms the epigraph of this book. I quote it below, and request you to read it with great attention:

> I closely observed his last facial expression, following his death. I did not understand anything. Not many understood this genius when he was alive. That includes me too. Even if we string together all our experiences, we will not be able to complete our study of him.

Ayyappa Paniker never desired for others to understand who he was. The belief that he must live like any other person in the company of fellow humans was second nature to him.

Priyadas G. Mangalath, the author of this book, recounts a small incident. As Ayyappa Paniker got ready to attend a poets' meet with one of his students, the student pointed out that the programme notice issued by the organisers did not include "Sir's" name. Paniker took the notice, read it, and, pointing to the phrase "and others" at the end of the list of participating poets, exclaimed, "There! That's my name!"

It may not be possible for others to have the same insight as Priyadas has to see this unique quality of Ayyappa Paniker's nature as indicative of the depth of his personality. Priyadas presents more detailed pictures of this special behavioural trait through several other observations. While going through all of them, the readers will surely be convinced that the extraordinariness of Ayyappa Paniker lay in his very ordinariness.

He knew fully well that the values of the commercial age had overpowered society completely. But he constantly rejected profit motives in his sphere of work. He was always willing to give his poems to fairly well-run publications, and through his activities he established that *Sankramanam*, the magazine brought out under Priyadas's leadership, was a part of his soul. The same applied to *Kerala Kavitha*.

To join the group of those who hoodwinked society by writing poems about commitment in a bid to win praises was unthinkable, as far as Ayyappa Paniker was concerned. He did not hesitate to take X-ray pictures of them either. In *"Mrityupuja"*, he says:

> When there is a war,
> or be it famine,
> he who lives for the people
> turns it to verse,
> and mints a little cash. ("Hymn to Death," trans. K.

Ayyappa Paniker, *Selected Poems of Ayyappa Paniker*, Modern Book Centre, 1985: 35)

(In fact, even his birth is "for the people"!)

Not many people will remember that even before such poems were compiled into an anthology, unfavourable critical pieces about them took a book form. But Ayyappa Paniker dismissed Thayat Sankaran's *Adhunika Kavithayude Jeerna Mukham* (The Decayed Face of Modernist Poetry) as mere childish prattle. (See the poem "*Pinnem Chankaran*".)

The idiom "*Pinnem Chankaran Thengelu*" ("Again, Chankaran is on the coconut palm") is a very profound usage. It indicates a moribund mind that not only does not perceive the change in sensibilities but sets out to criticize it as well. But no one will acknowledge that they themselves have such a retrograde attitude. It is difficult for stunted minds to see sprightliness in a line like "The present times are like a flat tyre" by Ayyappa Paniker.

Paniker viewed such people with utmost compassion. The title of the first poem in the anthology *Ayyappa Panikerude Kritikal* (Ayyappa Paniker's Works), published by Navadhara Publishing Cooperative Society, was "*Ente Bhithimel*" ("Upon My Walls").

Look at the picture my hands have drawn on my walls: Why do you stare? Look carefully, you fool! (trans. K. Ayyappa Paniker, *Selected Poems of Ayyappa Paniker*, Modern Book Centre, 1985: 9)

After showing clearly the very source of the picture he drew—using symbols that crystallized from his deep insight—Ayyappa Paniker uses the same lines to conclude the poem. His response to the viewer, who looks at it with a baffled expression, is one of pity. How else can one look at such a person? That was the nature of Ayyappa Paniker's humaneness. (The word "fool" only means a person who has not yet reached the level of new sensibility.)

The anthology contains "*Kurukshetram*" too, a poem written in 1957. Initially, the poem was not published by any magazine, and its copy was returned to the author. It is worth remembering that those editors who so unhesitatingly rejected the great work also belonged to the category of "fools".

The second part of the poem begins like this:

> When the devouring flames of fire and light
> erase the last traces of the dark blue clouds,
> and civilization closes its eyes,
> my soul wilts.
> Do you who read this know it,
> or don't you? ("*Kurukshetram*," trans. K. Ayyappa Paniker, *Selected Poems of Ayyappa Paniker*, Modern Book Centre, 1985: 17).

The poem encompasses the calamities that shook the soul of an era. The new sensibility that was required in order to appreciate it had only begun to sprout in the hearts of aesthetes. They need not be faulted for such lapses because "fools" are bound to overcome their limitations one day.

This generosity of spirit within Ayyappa Paniker, the poet, was vaster and profounder in Ayyappa Paniker, the human. And I respect Priyadas for his ability to look deep within and detect the core of Paniker's personality.

We cannot claim to have understood a person merely by assessing his or her heritage, circumstances of birth and growth, friends and relatives and so on. Only those who have insight, an almost mystical gift, will be able to understand the person at a deep level. By the word "understand", I mean recognising the personality or the soul of the subject.

For a very long time, I have felt that Priyadas has the clearest insight into Ayyappa Paniker the man, and this book emphatically endorses the correctness of my hunch (or impression).

This book, divided into 41 chapters, describes the various dimensions of Ayyappa Paniker's personality. Priyadas brings out the subtle aspects of his nature by vividly presenting concrete and poignant examples.

As a result, the person who appears in front of the eyes of the reader is a very unique individual who, not wishing the world to know of his creativity and goodness, concealed them deep inside the recesses of his soul. It is only in the concluding chapter that Priyadas quotes substantially from Ayyappa Paniker's poem "Epitaph":

> Here lies the body of Mister Panicker
> who at the end of his panicking days
> agreed to lie still for a while.
> It's not known what happened to his soul
> if indeed he ever had one.
> He wasn't quite unlike any of us while he lived:
> ....
> all his life he was patiently
> learning how not to live at all.

Very succinctly, Priyadas describes the ambit of his explorations, extending from Ayyappa Paniker's involvement in the presentation of plays to his involvement in the rehearsals; from reciting poetry to participating in poets' meetings; from the teacher's friendly warmth to the research guide's uncompromising sternness. It helps the readers take a peek into the sheer depths of his affection, which he assiduously sought to conceal. (Priyadas calls it "Self-masquerade".)

The manner in which Priyadas wraps up his work deserves special attention. He quotes Ayyappa Paniker's words:

> When we swim towards memories of old times, we become young. As we emerge from it, we forget old age. On remembering that, beyond a string of material and temporary losses, there are such fragrant loving moments in human life, many complaints about life are forgotten. Only that life is well-lived which allows memories of good things.

Ayyappa Paniker's soul throbs in these lines. The style, as always, is crystal clear. Through it, we get a glimpse of scenes that are beyond our normal range of vision.

Before I conclude, let me give in to the temptation of diving into the depths of my memory, and bringing out a small anecdote. Ayyappa Paniker and I went together by bus to Muvattupuzha to attend Priyadas's wedding. Priyadas and his wife Jessy would interact with Ayyappa Paniker very closely and in various ways in the years that followed, and I was aware of it. That bond has no place for separation and death. That is an immortal song. Let me withdraw, savouring the comfort of the pure sadness that has sedimented in my soul on reading this enjoyable book.

M.K. Sanoo

Preface

I WAS A student at Union Christian (UC) College, Aluva, in the state of Kerala, when I heard about Ayyappa Paniker, the poet, and read his poems for the first time. Later I got a chance to see him from afar, when he appeared at a poets' meet. Subsequently, on learning that this poet was a scholar of English language and literature and had translated many great literary works into Malayalam, a desire to become his student sprouted in my heart. Before long, I enrolled myself as a postgraduate student at the Institute of English, University of Kerala, Thiruvananthapuram, where he taught. This way, I could see him, listen to him and talk to him every day.

When I brought out *Sankramanam*, the little magazine, ran it for five years, launched a cassette of poetry and published books under the Sankramanam banner, I came to understand him better. Still later, when I pursued higher studies and went on to start various enterprises in order to make a living, I got more opportunities to interact and have discussions with him. Gradually, he became a constant presence, open or invisible, in my life and in nearly all the fields I worked in.

I spent time with him beyond the classroom, either at his house or mine, as well as at public venues, in India and abroad. I travelled a lot with him, getting on buses, trains and planes or in cars. I witnessed his various moods and saw him at close quarters in many stages of his life, especially in his last years.

Eventually, I felt I should write about the Ayyappa Paniker I had seen and known. That was also when I began to wonder whether there could be others who had had similar experiences to mine. There was little about him on the public domain because Ayyappa Paniker was a person who constantly turned down requests for interviews, saying, "My poems contain all that I have to say." Thus, in a bid to study him more deeply, I reread all his poems from a fresh perspective.

What you are about to read in the following pages is the result of my attempts to view Ayyappa Paniker through the prisms of his conversations, his actions and his writings.

There are several people who have proven their skills in the creative sphere, in the fields of arts, sports, employment or business, and gained renown through the media. In most cases, with longer association, our respect for them loses its sheen. I am not speaking about the experiences of fans who seek out autographs from or take selfies with their chosen celebrities. Rather, I am alluding to those who attempt to better understand people of merit in order to learn from their idols, and incorporate those lessons in their own lives. But viewed from closer quarters, it is not unusual for heroes to expose their clay feet.

It is possible to become famous and attract widespread attention through one's abilities, appearance, status or authority. It is also possible to capture eyeballs by mounting one's image on giant flex boards or filling the media space. But there are a few who choose to lead a quiet life, unnoticed by others, and go on with the ordinary business of living without loud displays of emotion. Rarer still are pure hearts who have unconditional love and empathy towards others.

As Ayyappa Paniker himself has said:

> How very generous —
> the buds of flame of human love
> on the seven-wick lamp
> that glows every twilight!

Thiruvananthapuram **Priyadas G. Mangalath**

Acknowledgements

THE SEED OF the idea that I should write about Ayyappa Paniker was sown in my mind years ago by M.K. Sanoo, the renowned Malayalam poet, critic, biographer and journalist. He won the central Sahitya Akademi Award in 2011. Later, I experienced the lines he wrote in *Ayyappa Panikerum Ayyappa Panikerum*, his book on Ayyappa Paniker, as a recurring reminder of the task I had set for myself:

> It is my belief that in the coming years, young generations caressing new dreams, will show their respect by writing ever new critical studies on that powerful personality whose light, like a diamond piercing the darkness, shone through the barrenness of a certain period of time.

When I began to seriously consider writing about Ayyappa Paniker, I informed Sanoo and kept him updated on the progress. His response was that as his eyes and ears were reminding him of approaching old age, expediting my work would be desirable. Once I completed the draft in Malayalam, I brought a printout to his home at Karikkamuri Road in Ernakulam. He immediately started reading it with a magnifying lens. Despite my assurances that he could take his time with the copy, he continued reading intently. After a while, he remarked, "It has come out fine. I am going to write about it."

Instantly, I had a thought: perhaps he should write an Introduction to my book. As a person and literary personality who had seen Ayyappa Paniker at very close quarters, Sanoo's endorsement of my experiential sketch was, in my eyes, absolutely essential. I am deeply grateful to him for blessing me with the Introduction.

Dr M.N. Rajan, the research supervisor and associate professor of the Department of Malayalam in the Government Women's College, Thiruvananthapuram and Dr Dominic J. Kattoor, the research supervisor and professor of the Department of Malayalam in the same college, went through the manuscript with the attention and seriousness of research guides.

I held discussions and cleared my doubts with Dr Rajan from time to time, and his reading through my work as though it were a thesis was a huge morale booster. Dr Dominic helped me by giving suggestions for the improvement of the draft, and Akhila Muralidharan of Altius, a youth movement to make the students of Kerala globally competent and socially committed, found time to proofread and correct it. A huge thank you to both of them.

Besides them, a few friends, who love and respect Ayyappa Paniker with as much or more fervour than I do, went through the text and gave me necessary directions and encouragement. My debt of gratitude to them as well as to you, the reader, for taking time to peruse this.

1
Union Christian College

READING WAS A passion for those who studied in the colleges of Kerala in the 1970s and '80s. When I joined Union Christian (UC) College, Aluva, for my undergraduate course, I was a great fan of English crime investigation novels. I was drawn into the world of Malayalam literature by my friends.

They spoke ceaselessly about writers such as O.V. Vijayan, Anand, K. Satchidanandan, Paul Zachariah, N.S. Madhavan, Sethu (A. Sethumadhavan), George Varghese Kakkanadan, Maniyambath Mukundan, M. Sukumaran, Vaikom Muhammad Basheer, Madhavikutty (Kamala Surayya/Das), T. Padmanabhan, V.P. Sivakumar, Kovilan (V.V. Ayyappan), Punathil Kunjabdulla and others, whipping up a huge zeal in me. As I began to read their literary works, and whenever they came up for discussion, there were references to Franz Kafka, Jean-Paul Sartre, Samuel Beckett, Albert Camus, Friedrich Nietzsche, Sigmund Freud, Carl Jung, Martin Heidegger, and so on. My subsequent journeys were along those paths. Once I fell under their spell, they began to haunt my days and nights.

Conversations with friends began to veer towards poetry most of the time. There were many who were interested in it and whenever we got together, they recited poems. Modernism became a hot topic of discussion and it was precisely for that reason that only the poems composed by modernist poets of that time were recited. In this manner, an interest in poetry was born in me.

As a school student, I had little appreciation for poetry; metres like *Keka, Kaakali, Indravajra, Shardoolavikreeditham* and others made my head spin. I would memorize the prescribed poems and recite them mechanically when asked by teachers, but my heart was never in it. My friends introduced me to modernist poetry, which did not follow any metrical pattern but was powered by the rhythm of prose. I began to grow fond of reading and listening to modernist poems. Poetry became an intoxicant at formal and informal student gatherings, drawing us into spontaneous assemblies beneath the shady trees of the college premises. The most popular poets were Kadammanitta (M.R. Ramakrishna Panikkar), Kunjunni Mash, Ayyappa Paniker, Sugathakumari, K. Satchidanandan and D. Vinayachandran.

The craze for modernist poetry became a mainstream preoccupation in campuses because of many factors. A modernist poem could be memorised partially or fully, and recited loudly whenever the urge kicked in. Listeners quickly flocked to the spot, and the renditions did not take long. It was sometimes possible to recite a full Kunjunni poem or an Ayyappa Paniker composition within the span of time we took to walk from one classroom to another. One could listen to it and get time to express one's appreciation too. (The General English classes were held in different buildings within the vast campus of UC College.) There were plenty of occasions for such recitals—during the recess, the afternoon hours or even a period when the teacher concerned did not turn up. (Other genres, like the short story, took more time to read or summarize.) The uniqueness of the styles of recitation also made poetry more popular.

Kadammanitta's *"Shanta"*, Ayyappa Paniker's *"Sandhya"* (as the segment "October 10–15" in *"Pakalukal Rathrikal"* ["Days and Nights"] was more popularly known in the campuses), Satchidanandan's *"Kozhipanku"* or Sugathakumari's *"Rathrimazha"*—recited by the poets themselves and repeated by students at countless gatherings—still echo in my memory today. That generation of modernist writers were virtually entwined to our souls with hoops of steel. As writers who had composed works that helped establish modernism in the cultural landscape of Kerala, Ayyappa Paniker, the poet, and O.V. Vijayan, the short story writer, commanded special respect.

Besides, the articles by Narendra Prasad, K.P. Appan, M. Thomas Mathew and others presented the modernist writers as architects of the new age. This was done in full recognition of and deep regard for figures such as Edasseri Govindan Nair, Vyloppilli Sreedhara Menon and Vaikom Muhammad Basheer whose status as outliers remain undisputed even today.

As soon as new artistic works hit the stands, interested people gathered together to exchange views. In the case of poetry, recitations also took place. Debates, big and small, on works that were based on philosophical schools of thought, including existentialism, happened inside the classrooms and outside. Modernist writers like M. Govindan convincingly argued that life is not a set of maudlin moods that hooks youth to daydreams. Rather, it is up to us to enrich our existence by infusing meaning into the singular experience of life. Generally speaking, everybody showed an affinity towards the neglected. Although many teachers of UC College—especially Dr K.V. Kunjikrishnan of the Department of History or O.A. Abraham of the Department of Malayalam—never taught me, they stood strongly by me in the political and literary stances I took, and this continues to impart vibrancy to my recollections of those times.

Literature and politics were two subjects that consumed considerable time of the students. In those days, there were many students in UC College who maintained a close affiliation with left extremist thought. For sympathizers of existentialism, who believed that individual freedom was paramount, opposition to the Emergency was only a short step away. The protest spread like wild fire. But whatever the form of opposition, the quotient of literature in it, especially poetry, was very high. Lines from many poems, like Ayyappa Paniker's *"Kadukka"* ("Gallnut"), for instance, that were penned against the backdrop of the Emergency, were etched deep in the memory of most students.

What I mean to say is that poets exercised a great deal of influence during that period. And among them, Ayyappa Paniker was hugely respected. Students could easily recite from memory, lines from his works like *"Kurukshetram"*, *"Kudumbapuranam"* ("The Family Saga"), *"Mrityupuja"* ("Hymn to Death"), *"Martyapuja"* ("Hymn to Man"), *"Agnipuja"* ("Fire Worship"), "Hey, Gagarin!", *"Pakalukal Rathrikal"* ("Days and Nights") and others. His compositions exhibited a startling variety, and for that reason his poems appealed to a wide spectrum of poetry enthusiasts.

Sometime during this period, under pressure from my parents, although I nursed dreams about taking my postgraduate degree from Jawaharlal Nehru University (JNU), Delhi, when it came to selecting a college, the Institute of English (under the University of Kerala) where Ayyappa Paniker taught was my confirmed choice.

That a famous Malayalam poet had earned his doctoral degree in English literature (that too, from a land where English was the mother tongue!) and was teaching it, tickled my fancy in no small measure. I also heard that although he wrote articles, delivered speeches and took classes in English, when it came to composing poetry, Malayalam was his preferred tongue. That remained a conundrum in the minds of students during debates in the campus. (Madhavikutty,[1] who wrote poems in English and stories in Malayalam, used to be discussed too.)

Ayyappa Paniker was hailed as a person who had liberated Malayalam poetry from the vice-like grip of those who insisted that only metrical lines counted as true verse. He earned the sobriquet of "the spiritual master of Malayalam poetry"—and all these factors enhanced his star value.

It was in this manner that Ayyappa Paniker drew me towards Thiruvananthapuram.

---

1 More popularly known as Kamala Das (1934–2009) among English readers.

2
The Institute of English

I DID NOT possess any poetic skills. Nor did I desire to take up teaching as a career. Yet I came to the Institute of English in Thiruvananthapuram in order to become Ayyappa Paniker's student although the logic for that decision is utterly unknown to me, to this day.

Climbing the steps to the first floor of the Institute of English and entering my classroom, my mind was full of the image of the most recognised poet-translator-scholar in Malayalam who had drunk deep from the Pierian spring of English literature (the fountain of Macedonia that was sacred to the Muses and a source of inspiration). Whom I saw instead was an ordinary teacher.

I imagined he would make references to Malayalam poetry and his own compositions. But nothing of that kind happened. I expected that, since he had taken his Master of Arts (MA) and PhD degrees from America, he would speak about his life in the US, and the poets he met there. That did not happen either. He did not even drop a hint that he had studied in America, or earned any degree from that land. Statements like "When I was in Indiana University …" uttered in jest or in passing, never fell from his lips. What I saw instead was the unpretentiousness of a Kuttanad[1] farmer.

A soft voice and an informality of behaviour were his hallmarks. Gradually, I came to realize that humility was not a superficial ornament he wore. It was a special and organic quality that, perhaps unknown even to himself, informed his talk, his actions and his very appearance.

During our first year, he taught us American literature. Ralph Waldo Emerson, Henry David Thoreau, Walt Whitman and Emily Dickinson affected me deeply. I felt they were his favourites. As Thoreau, who gained a gigantic stature through his simple living, and Emerson, whose thoughts lay close to Indian philosophy, reached us through Ayyappa Paniker, they became dear to us. When Ayyappa Paniker taught Whitman's "Passage to India", I thought he would speak about his own poem titled "Passage to America", penned during his stay in the US in 1970. He did not. Later, in 1982, his poem "*Innale Njaan Whitmane Kandu*" ("I Met Whitman Yesterday") appeared in *Kala Kaumudi*, a weekly news magazine published in Malayalam in Kerala. I read

---

1 A region covering Alappuzha, Kottayam and Pathanamthitta districts, it is known to be the granary of Kerala.

it greedily probably because I was reminded of Ayyappa Paniker's classes on Whitman and his poetry.

Ayyappa Paniker did not have a traditional approach to teaching. There were no flamboyant or majestic-sounding speeches. His sentences were crisp and simple and his glances were searching, his minimalist sentences and gestures appearing to justify his scanning look. Giving notes or explaining texts exhaustively was not his style. Most of the time, his jokes were not very transparent, so I had difficulty grasping them quickly, especially in the initial days. (Once, when I asked a classmate why she did not laugh at Ayyappa Paniker's jokes, her reply was, "I have to think about what he said, and by the time I discover the meaning, I can laugh only the next day!")

One had to be wary of veiled barbs that lay concealed in the jokes he cracked at unexpected moments. He lost his temper very rarely and most of the time, his face looked cheerful. He did not dictate but gave only suggestions so that those who were interested could be guided by them, and move forward. As this was an unusual method, like many other students who had come from various colleges in Kerala, I took some time to follow his pedagogical style. Although he adopted a more serious approach towards research scholars, he was generally lenient with his MA students.

When we went on a picnic, it was Ayyappa Paniker who accompanied us. We drove to Ponmudi, a hilly region about 55 kilometres from Thiruvananthapuram city. The valleys that appeared within view as our bus navigated hairpin bends were fabulous. Ayyappa Paniker's presence and proximity was no hindrance to the freedom we enjoyed throughout the trip. Instead of the gravity associated with higher studies, what we experienced was the warmth and softness of his friendship. He viewed us as mature adults, capable of taking our own decisions, and ready to shoulder the responsibilities that came in their wake. When cross-gender friendships bloomed among us, Ayyappa Paniker did not grow anxious like a conservative guardian. He did not show the dislike or anger of the moral police because he perceived us as grown-ups. Maybe that was the reason, we heard, he was the teacher who invariably accompanied students on such pleasure trips.

For most teachers, relationships with students does not extend beyond the classroom, the bond between the teacher and the taught invariably staying confined to the classroom or the college premises. Outside the campus, the friendship usually freezes into a formal contact. Certainly, there are exceptions, and Ayyappa Paniker, the *guru*, epitomised the unique beauty of such a special bond.

I know for sure that none of my classmates have visited the homes of their teachers, but I am doubly sure that it would be a rare student of the Institute of English who had not gone to Ayyappa Paniker's house. It was customary for him to formally invite all his students to his house during the last month of their postgraduate course at the Institute. He would prepare all the dishes, and serve them to each individual student. That gesture gave us the authentic fragrance and taste of the *gurukulam* system of education when the student was closely guided by the teacher and sometimes even lived in the same house. It was so expressive that every student could sense that he would be by their side always, ready to offer help or give advice when required. The message was taken even without Ayyappa Paniker articulating it. Even otherwise, it was not in his nature to spell out everything specifically. These annual "home visits" at the end of the course continued like a ritual, without a break.

What were the benefits of studying at the Institute of English? I could see Ayyappa Paniker every single day. Although I skipped the classes of many other teachers, I do not recall ever missing a single one he held. I observed his gait and his glances, I experienced his laughter and his happiness, and I enjoyed his light and dark humour, all at close quarters. The wealth I absorbed from the informal Ayyappa Paniker outside the classroom beggars whatever I learnt at his feet inside the formal walls of the Institute of English.

3
The Time of Transition[1]

WHEN THE MAINSTREAM media in Kerala slow-pedalled in updating the new generations about the changes in Malayalam literature and culture that were upturning old prejudices and traditional approaches, little magazines stepped in, considering it their duty to take up that responsibility. *Sankramanam* (literally meaning "Transition")

---

1 The word "Transition" refers to at least three phenomena, which are interconnected and also linked to my (the author's) life. One, it is the meaning of the little magazine *Sankramanam* of which I was the founder-editor. Two, its publication coincided with a change in the literary sensibility of both the intellectuals and the public in Kerala, as they transitioned from the orthodoxy of traditional norms to the laissez-faire culture of modernism. Three, the patronage of Ayyappa Paniker brought about a sustained and deep interaction with my mentor, causing a transition in my own intellectual and personal life.

was a social and cultural publication that joined the ranks of *Sameeksha, Yugarashmi, Anweshanam, Kerala Kavitha, Jwala* and others. But it went a step further, and published books as well as anthologies of poetry. During those days, several artists and youngsters who were advocates of modernism were enthusiastic participants in the *Sankramana Sandhya* programmes (poetry-reading sessions) that were conducted at various places, in association with the release of the latest issue of *Sankramanam*.

The first issue of *Sankramanam* came out while I was doing my MA at the Institute of English. It was published every month, though not at regular intervals, and, in all, more than 50 issues were published from 1978 to 1984. It was started under the initiative of K.N. Shaji, who was my junior in UC College and became its chief editor. The editorial board included Apsalan Vathussery, Maupassant Vallath, Balachandran Chullikkad, Venu V. Desam and myself. After a few months, however, Shaji went on a sabbatical, left the *Sankramanam* team and much later, started another magazine called *Niyogam*. Three months after the launch of *Sankramanam*, its publication was shifted from Aluva to Thiruvananthapuram. As P.K. Rajasekharan, a critic, wrote in *Pakshikkoottangal*, his study of little magazines, "As soon as the publication of *Sankramanam* was shifted to Thiruvananthapuram, it underwent a great transition" (Kerala Media Academy, 2021: 184).

My living quarters—Room number 17 in Ashoka Lodge at Spencer Junction, opposite the University College, Thiruvananthapuram—became the office of *Sankramanam*.

That the same lodge was the birthplace of *Aksharam*, the little magazine begun by the poet Ayyappan in 1973, was a matter of pure coincidence and my decision to roost on Ashoka, which provided a perch for those interested in reading and literary discussions, was merely fortuitous. The room had only enough space for a cot, a table and a chair, but that did not come in the way of accommodating guests if they were prepared to adjust to the circumstances. As the lodge was situated in the heart of the city, writers and other friends who were subscribers of *Sankramanam* found it convenient to come and go as they pleased.

When a few members of the editorial board left, new ones shouldered the responsibilities. The services of K.X. Raju, who had been my classmate at UC College, were available all the time. V.K. Unnikrishnan, who was employed at the office of the University of Kerala, pitched in whenever he could. There were several others who extended a lot of support, the most noteworthy among them being Renji Panicker who would go on to become a screenplay writer, film director and actor. He not only contributed poems and articles under the name "K. Renji" but cooperated hugely and wholeheartedly to bring out *Sankramanam*, doing the editing work as well.

During those days a man named John C., who ran a small business in the Palayam market nearby, used to come to Ashoka Lodge every day to meet a friend of his. An industrious man with a lot of practical wisdom, John C. was not greatly interested in literature or education, but he watched our *Sankramanam* activities with keen interest. We soon made him our business manager because it eased our path towards taking loans. However, he went beyond his call of duty, helped out in the sale and distribution of *Sankramanam*, and thus guaranteed its continued existence. I gratefully recall the help he rendered and the cooperation he extended. Today he is the proprietor of Variety Mall in Thiruvananthapuram city that sells beauty products for women, and enjoys a rich clientele.

Although M. Krishnan Nair[2] was no great fan of modernist literature and although we never solicited articles from him, he would drop in at the lodge on most evenings before he proceeded to the Indian Coffee House. As he spoke about world writers and their works, we listened with great enthusiasm.

The persons who contributed the most to *Sankramanam* were Ayyappa Paniker and G. Aravindan.[3] At one stage, the last page of the magazine always carried a cartoon by Aravindan. Later, K.K. Balaraman, a student of journalism at the Kariavattom campus of the University of Kerala, contributed his cartoons, and they attracted critical

---

2 M. Krishnan Nair (1923–2006) was a well-known orator and literary critic of Malayalam literature. His weekly column "Sahitya Vaaraphalam", that ran for several decades, was instrumental in introducing global writers to Kerala's literary community and popularizing their work.

3 G. Aravindan (1935–91) was a famous film director, screenplay writer, cartoonist and painter. He won recognition as a film director at the state and national levels, and was awarded the prestigious Padma Shri in 1990. Some of his well-known films are *Uttarayanam, Kanchana Sita, Thampu, Chidambaram* and *Vasthuhara*.

attention. Ayyappa Paniker's poems, translations and articles lent a respectable dimension to *Sankramanam* in the eyes of literature enthusiasts. Pradeep Panangad, the cultural historian who has made a mark in the field of new media, commented in his book titled *Malayala Samanthara Masika Charitram* (The History of Parallel Magazines in Malayalam): "*Sankramanam* could create new stars in the wide skies of Modernism in Malayalam. It always attempted to open doors to the new world of literature. For that reason, proponents of Modernism like Ayyappa Paniker showed a special affinity towards *Sankramanam*" (Kerala Bhasha Institute, 2018: 220).

What filled the *Sankramanam* team with a deep sense of gratification was that alongside contributing creative pieces to it, Ayyappa Paniker went through each and every issue. As soon as the printing and binding of the magazine was over, we took it to him. I also remember going to the houses of Aravindan, K.S. Narayana Pillai, Narendra Prasad, V.P. Sivakumar and others in association with *Sankramanam*. We did not send a single issue to Ayyappa Paniker by post. Even when the number of subscribers mounted to 5,000, we took each issue, and handed it personally to him. Then we waited for his evaluation. His glancing through it constituted a certificate of approval, as far as we were concerned. Whenever we faced setbacks or felt low, his certification worked as a shot in the arm. The positive strokes given by him and other writers held us from collapsing, and encouraged us to march forward. M.K. Sanoo writes about the conversation he once had with Ayyappa Paniker in the course of a trip:

One of the topics of conversation was *Sankramanam*, edited by Priyadas. He spoke seriously about the need to not only compliment the creative contributions made by *Sankramanam* in drawing readers closer to the changes taking place on the plane of sensibility in literature but extend all possible support as well. Editorial responsibilities were discharged without any fanfare. A smooth and seamless transition of sensibility was facilitated. These were the two virtues of *Sankramanam* he highlighted. He also reminded me that all of us were obliged to give it all the help we were capable of. He fulfilled his duties in this regard. As a result, the magazine succeeded in acquiring a unique identity and making unique contributions to our culture.

Personal and idealistic dimensions were very dominant in the relationship between Ayyappa Paniker and Priyadas. In general, it was a similar relationship that he (Ayyappa Paniker) maintained with others too. (*Ayyappa Panikerum Ayyappa Panikerum* [Ayyappa Paniker and Ayyappa Paniker], Green Books, 2014: 12).

The 1980s marked a transition from modernism to postmodernism. Therefore, topics related to it got reflected in nearly all the discussions we had with Ayyappa Paniker. Keen readers of *Sankramanam* could detect this subtle shift in sensibility in most of the poems the magazine carried.

After class hours, Ayyappa Paniker used to walk from the Institute of English, situated behind the office complex of the University of Kerala, towards the main road from where he took an autorickshaw to go home. On many days, I joined him on some pretext or another as he walked the distance. Once when our conversation happened to touch upon the poems in *Sankramanam* that conveyed the shift in literary sensibility, I mentioned my wish to collect and publish them in an anthology. Immediately, he suggested its title—*Aadhunikothara Kavitha* (Postmodern Poems). He saw that I was terribly excited. But a few days later, when we walked the same route, he observed that my spirits had become somewhat dull. He asked me when the book would get published. I reluctantly had to admit that paucity of funds was a major hurdle. In reply, Ayyappa Paniker casually mentioned that he would sound the idea with D.C. Kizhakemuri.[4] The next day, when I went to the Institute, Ayyappa Paniker told me that he had settled the matter with DC Books. The expenses would be taken care of, the firm would publish and sell copies of the book, retrieve its investment, and offer the rest of the profits to me. If this condition was acceptable, I could hand over the material to the firm! A month after I sent the matter, the book was published by DC Books. *Kala Kaumudi* carried an advertisement of the book without charging me anything. (Let me take this opportunity to thank the editors S. Jayachandran Nair and N.R.S. Babu for their generosity.) Within a very short period of time, 1,000 copies of *Aadhunikothara Kavitha* were sold.

---

4 D.C. Kizhakemuri (1914–99) was a prominent book publisher and the owner of DC Books.

I slowly began to experience how, even while remaining my teacher, Ayyappa Paniker had shapeshifted to become my mentor. Not only did he not allow a wish of mine to remain a pipe dream and get snuffed out eventually, he encouraged me to go ahead with it, and even lent his hand to make *Aadhunikothara Kavitha* a tangible reality for me. With the publication of this book, the cash-strapped *Sankramanam* magazine gained a certain gravitas, got more subscribers, and carved a special and serious place for itself in readers' forums as well as in their minds.

4
John Abraham

ALTHOUGH *AGRAHARATHIL KAZHUTHAI* (Donkey in a Brahmin Village) was a Tamil film, when it won the national award in 1977, its director John Abraham received great recognition all over Kerala. Even before he was awarded, many stories and tall tales about him had circulated widely, and made him a legend in popular imagination. Since that film caused uneasiness among the conservatives and celebrated the spirit of modernism, and also because John was an iconoclast, the youth of Kerala celebrated his success everywhere. John's next film *Cheriyaachante Kroora Krityangal* (The Evil Deeds of Cheriyachan) also challenged existing notions about films.

One day, after the shooting of the film was over, I was introduced to John at the poet Kadammanitta's residence at Pipinmoodu. As I stepped into the room, I saw John sitting on Kadammanitta's cot, talking to him. John's hair and beard were overgrown, and it seemed that he had not had a bath in a long time.

Maybe because he had not seen me earlier, John stared hard and long at me. Finally, breaking his silence, he asked hesitantly and doubtfully, "Am I sitting or standing?" For the first time in my life, I became conscious about my own similar state of hirsute richness, although no one had commented on it until then.

Our friendship subsequently grew and deepened. For some time thereafter, Ashoka–17, Spencer Junction, Thiruvananthapuram 691 001 was not only the office of *Sankramanam* and my living quarters, but became John's bedroom as well. His main food was liquor. Alcoholism had become a popular fad among artists and writers. Besides, wearing clean clothes and leading a disciplined life were not habits patronised by many intellectuals in those days. Many of the gifted poets and short story writers of the modern era were either full-time or part-time tipplers. And this long list of eggheads influenced thinking and non-thinking youngsters, alike.

John's statements were rich in philosophy and appropriate quotes. He can be given credit or faulted for spreading a kind of anarchic intellectual culture throughout Kerala. Although he was a genius, not all his imitators could lay claim to that virtue. He had original ideas not only about films but about music and literature as well. John had established his genuine talent through his films and short stories. It was he who wrote the Introduction to *Aadhunikothara Kavitha*, the first publication of Sankramanam. He wrote stories for *Sankramanam* magazine, and cooperated in editorial activities too. He constantly spoke about gifted film directors like Ritwik Ghatak and others and about good films. John exercised no self-control over his talk, but that was the John his admirers liked. However, no one had seen him maintaining any discipline. That the residents of Ashoka Lodge endured, permitted and appreciated the poetry sessions that he and Kadammanitta conducted at Ashoka–17 on many nights was a measure of the popularity both of them enjoyed not merely in Thiruvananthapuram but the whole of Kerala at that period of time.

The conversations that John and Aravindan had whenever they met were very engaging. That was because most of the time, Aravindan's replies were mere grunts. Such a response was not only because John was inebriated but due to the fact that by nature, Aravindan was a man of few words. Most people jokingly remarked that Aravindan's films were experiments with silence.

John wished to meet Ayyappa Paniker and talk to him. But he feared that appearing in front of Ayyappa Paniker in a state of alcoholic stupor would be disrespectful. Therefore, although the two geniuses acknowledged each other, their meetings were relatively rare.

One day, John expressed his desire to visit Ayyappa Paniker. The time and date of the meeting was decided upon, and permission sought. On the appointed day, John joined me and we set out. But as he had consumed too much liquor, I felt uneasy so I suggested that we postpone the meeting. Replying that going back on the word given to

Ayyappa Paniker would be a worse crime, he walked with me to the Institute.

On the way, however, John tripped over a stone and fell down. Maybe because he feared his stagger would be slower or because he was in pain, John told me, "You proceed. I'm not coming today since I fell ..." Feeling relieved, I continued to walk and went to the Institute. I knocked at Ayyappa Paniker's door, stepped into his room, and sat on the chair he indicated.

"Didn't John say he would come? I thought you would come together. You stay in the same place, don't you?" Ayyappa Paniker asked.

"Yes. We stay together and set out together. But John tripped and fell on the way. Although he clambered back to his feet, he asked me to proceed. He had drunk a little ...," I managed to say.

"Can't he do without liquor? Does he need it all the time?"

"24 x 7."

Without uttering another word, either about John or his drinking habit, Ayyappa Paniker turned to talking about *Aadhunikothara Kavitha*.

A little later, someone knocked at the door. Ayyappa Paniker said loudly, "Come in!"

When I turned back, I was shell-shocked. It was John Abraham himself!

"Oh! The fallen Abraham has arrived!" Ayyappa Paniker gestured him to a chair.

We laughed at Ayyappa Paniker's humour. (Several variants, interpretations and editions of this episode got circulated in the course of time, with slight alterations in the setting and context of the action.)

That day, the conversation between Ayyappa Paniker and John, humorous and serious by turns, went on for more than half an hour and I was left wondering where John's drunkenness had disappeared. I had never thought John was capable of speaking in a sober fashion. He sat in front of Ayyappa Paniker like an obedient student, his words and gestures appropriately decorous!

Later, on many an occasion, I was an active participant in or a witness to the conversations between these two brilliant minds and every time, without fail, I saw and experienced the sharp wit of the one grind against the whetstone of the other, sending bright sparks all over the place. I saw the fiery spirit of intoxication getting doused too. But never once did I hear Ayyappa Paniker advising John to tone down his alcohol addiction. (My pontifications on the subject had met with wholesome scorn but, let me admit, after a few weeks, as long as he stayed with me at Ashoka–17, John kept away from liquor and led a normal life.)

I could understand the sobriety of Narendra Prasad, Kadammanitta and Vinayachandran. That was because although they drank heavily, they were not enslaved to the habit. However, what amazed me was that the poet Ayyappan, who cared for no one in the world, always took care to behave respectably and respectfully in front of Ayyappa Paniker!

5
"A Person Unknown to Me"

IT WAS DECIDED that the October 1980 issue of *Sankramanam* should be released in Bangalore. Writer and critic U.R. Ananthamurthy and the poet P. Lankesh had readily agreed to participate in the function. Also, Ayyappa Paniker from Kerala.

At the start of the trip, I reached the railway station early. Ayyappa Paniker joined me soon afterwards. The agent who had been entrusted with the task of arranging tickets for us awaited us there. (In those days, it was usual for people to give the responsibility of booking tickets to agents.) He handed over the tickets to us and apologised as sleeping berths were not available even though the Thiruvananthapuram–Bangalore journey was an overnight one. The chief guest of the *Sankramana Sandhya* organised at Bangalore, who was supposed to take a flight, was now waiting at the railway station in Thiruvananthapuram, with no prospect of even stretching his limbs on a berth!

Ayyappa Paniker, seeing stress and sadness congeal on my face, patted me on my back, and said with a smile, "It doesn't matter." He continued to crack jokes till our train pulled into the station. We got on the train and took our seats. Soon, the ticket examiner came and checked our tickets. We explained our situation to him. Maybe because he recognised Ayyappa Paniker, the gentleman engaged us in small talk. Then some time later, he arranged a sleeping berth for Ayyappa Paniker, and another for me afterwards.

When, in 1990, Ayyappa Paniker retired at the age of 60 from the University of Kerala, a send-off function was organised at the Town Hall in Thiruvananthapuram. A very distinguished panel of guests was present at the function—the governor, the minister for cultural affairs, Madhavikutty (the writer, Kamala Das), M.V. Devan (the painter, sculptor and art critic), M.K. Sanoo, Dr G.B. Balamohan Thampi, an academic, author and former vice chancellor of the University of Kerala, and others. In his reply speech, alluding to the praises showered on him, Ayyappa Paniker remarked, "Thank you for all the good words that were uttered here about a person unknown to me. As you know, it is always delightful to hear good words said about anyone."

Ayyappa Paniker did not speak long. Although he found it extremely difficult to listen to people praising him, he endured it all, and concluded his speech by quoting a few lines from a poem he had written ridiculing *Shashtipoorthi* (the 60th birth anniversary) celebrations.

Shashtipoorthi

> My grand *Shashtipoorthi* festival,
> Long live my *Shashtipoorthi*!
> ... ...
> Let me lose not the potency imparted
> by life's first *Shashtipoorthi*:
> Let me sing tunefully
> the statement about my part:
> My grand *Shashtipoorthi* festival
> Victory to *Shashtipoorthi* hereafter too!

Although Ayyappa Paniker was a significant member of the cultural sphere in Kerala, he did not perceive himself in that light. For that reason, he kept away from the formalities and fanfare that accompanied such a status. Once, while he was still teaching at the Institute, he asked a poet-student of his to meet him after class hours. The student replied that as he had to attend a poets' meet at the Town Hall and recite a poem, he had to leave early. Ayyappa Paniker remarked that he too would be participating in it, and suggested that they go to the venue together. The young poet whipped out the programme sheet and, after confirming that Ayyappa Paniker's name was not mentioned in the list, showed it to him. Ayyappa Paniker confidently assured the young man that he could point out his name, took the notice into his hands, and indicating a spot, said, "There! That's my name." The programme sheet had a list of names of several poets, at the end of which was the phrase "and others"—and that was what Ayyappa Paniker had pointed to!

Even when he experienced the comforts of the state-of-the-art technology that the modern world provided, Ayyappa Paniker led a simple life. Like Leonardo da Vinci, he considered simplicity to be the ultimate sophistication. It was not that he rejected luxury—rather, he did not go after it. It was not that he preferred to lie on a mat spread on the floor or on a coir cot without a mattress on it, but enjoyed to the fullest whatever was served to him. Although *Sankramanam* carried more than 15 poems of Ayyappa Paniker and an equal number of his other compositions, they were given only as much importance as the rest of the pieces.

At this point, I am reminded of what Lalitha Lenin, the poet, recalled in *Kerala Kavitha* about her first glimpse of Ayyappa Paniker:

> A poets' meet was organised at University College in Thiruvananthapuram in 1980. After the programme, when I saw young poets surround Ayyappa Paniker and accompany him right up to the Institute of English, I was astounded. I realised Ayyappa Paniker was the brightest celebrity at that time (2007: 246).

6
Prize Money

AYYAPPA PANIKER KNEW fully well that composing literary works alone did not constitute cultural activities. He was aware that it took several factors like film-making, theatre and book publication—enterprises that involved money and team work—to make the cultural field vibrant and rich. And he placed a great premium on the people involved in such cultural activities. As a result, most of the little magazines in Malayalam enjoyed his warm support. All book publishers, big and small, have experienced the cordiality of his generous cooperation.

In olden times, utterances were popular and powerful possibly because the written word had not come into being. Yet, even today, recited poems impart a kind of enjoyment that is very unique. One may fail to grasp the meaning of an occasional word or two but the subtle nuances of the uttered poetic sounds have a way of entering one's very bloodstream. That was the reason why modernist poems could set the college campuses in Kerala on fire in the 1970s and '80s with recitals and performances.

During that period, the *Sankramanam* team considered recording the poets' recitals of their own compositions, and taking the audio cassettes to poetry enthusiasts all over Kerala. We discussed the idea with Ayyappa Paniker. And wasn't he always on the side of new experiments and novel experiences!

He himself spoke to Kulathoor Bhaskaran Nair, the renowned producer of Malayalam films, and arranged facilities at the Chitralekha Sound Recording Studio. The first audio cassette that we brought out was of an hour's duration, and carried Ayyappa Paniker's rendering of his "*Pakalukal Rathrikal*" ("Days and Nights") and "*Mrityupuja*" ("Hymn to Death"). Kadammanitta recited "*Devisthavam*", "*Kurathi*" and "*Kaattaalan*". In 1980, when neither CDs nor the internet had made their appearance, this experiment was given a rousing welcome by poetry lovers.

Ayyappa Paniker was very conscious of the fact that it was our love for poetry and literature that inspired us to embark on such risky projects. When the Sankramanam book publishing enterprise was started, and discussions were held about which books to choose and how to proceed, Ayyappa Paniker cooperated with us by getting in touch with various writers and getting them to participate in the venture. It was he who selected the poems for our anthology titled *Kaviyarangu*. When more and more people started buying it, instead of asking for remuneration (as many other poets did), what Ayyappa Paniker did was to reassure us. "Now you can start repaying the loan you had taken to publish the book," he said.

He encouraged us in every enterprise related to *Sankramanam*, and gave us all the necessary guidelines. Never once did he ask for or even desire anything in return. That fact fills me with energy even today.

But this was not a closeness that Ayyappa Paniker reserved exclusively for *Sankramanam*. Everyone who went to him in order to discuss literary ventures and the finances involved in them, experienced this streak of ascetic detachment in his attitude towards money. For example, Dr M.R. Thampan, the director of Kerala Bhasha Institute, used to visit Ayyappa Paniker every morning in connection with the publication of the fifth volume of a literary encyclopaedia. Although it began as a session for merely clearing doubts, those morning meetings continued for a long period, with Ayyappa Paniker supervising the making of the entire volume, right up to its last page. Finally, when the book was about to be printed, permission was sought to insert Ayyappa Paniker's name as the guest editor. Ayyappa Paniker tried to dissuade Dr Thampan, arguing that he had not contributed a great amount to deserve that title, but had to relent when Dr Thampan's pressure became strong and persistent. In the course of time, the book got published, and one day Dr Thampan appeared at Ayyappa Paniker's house carrying a copy of the encyclopaedia as well as a cheque for a decent amount. Ayyappa Paniker cordially declined the cheque stating that he had not done enough to earn the remuneration! Recounting this incident, Dr Thampan remarked that he had never come across such a person ever in his entire life.

Many editors and publishers have mentioned that it was not Ayyappa Paniker's habit to accept money for his compositions or books. There are other stories too, of people sending him remuneration without seeking his consent and sometimes even discounting his opinion! In a nutshell, Ayyappa Paniker was not willing to haggle in the name of his creativity.

The following lines from "*Mrityupuja*" ("Hymn to Death") epitomise his perspective:

> When there is a war
> or be it famine,
> he who lives for the people
> turns it to verse,
> and mints a little cash.

Ayyappa Paniker's works were published for the first time in 1974. The publisher was Navadhara. The head of the Navadhara Publishing Cooperative Society, E.N. Muralidharan Nair, later became Chief Minister E.K. Nayanar's private secretary. It was Navadhara itself that first published *Marana Certificate* (Death Certificate) by the writer, Anand, and M. Mukundan's *Anchara Vayassulla Kutty* (A Five-and-a-half-year-old Child). Muralidharan Nair was an aesthete who recognised that great literary activity was not confined to writing alone but included efforts to offer well-written works and introduce a novel sensibility to the readers. Therefore, he considered the publication of books as an artistic project. Ayyappa Paniker gave his poems to Navadhara, stating at the very outset that he did not want any royalty. Many modernist writers shared the same thought. But when the anthology of poems won the Kerala Sahitya Akademi Award, Ayyappa Paniker rang up Muralidharan Nair, and said something that the latter found difficult to believe, "The work received the award because you published it. Let Navadhara keep the prize money. Don't reveal this to anyone though" (*Kerala Kavitha*, 2007: 176).

Others who have interacted with Ayyappa Paniker may have more heartwarming stories to relate regarding his monkish disregard for money.

7
One Hundred Per Cent

ON COMPLETING MY MA course, I began to think of doing research under Ayyappa Paniker. The subject we considered for my work was black humour. Although ours was a teacher student relationship, outside the Institute of English I enjoyed a lot of freedom and opportunity to discuss matters apart from academic subjects, like literary, cultural, political and social issues. During such sessions, Ayyappa Paniker cracked more jokes and passed comments without any reservations either about his age or his status. Later, I decided not to carry out research under him for fear that I would lose this freedom that had blossomed in our friendship. Subsequently, I signed up for a Master's course in journalism at the Karyavattom campus of the University of Kerala.

Ayyappa Paniker was not a person to be content with anything that fell below one hundred per cent. There were many students who registered themselves as PhD candidates under him, totally unaware of this looming challenge, and others like me who consciously avoided the dangerous situation. However, a majority of students did not evade him but rather worked really hard to earn their doctoral degrees under his supervision. Dhanya Menon who jumped into the deep end, despite being forewarned and fobbed off by danger signals, had this to say of her experiences:

> ... he warned me, "I might make life miserable for you, you better think twice ... I'll make you run around to discuss new topics and chapters ... in fact, you'll regret your decision throughout your life. Are you still ready for the game?"
>
> I agreed. I wanted to be his student, and nothing else mattered.
>
> The topic was selected and our sessions together became more serious and more frequent. My weekend trips to Thrissur came to a complete standstill and were replaced by hours in the university library. He used to call up in the dead of night to discuss the possibilities of including some text in one of the chapters and expected me to be awake and ready with pen and paper at 1 a.m. without appearing to be groggy or confused. "Include all these points, get it typed and bring it to my office at 10 tomorrow."
>
> Period. That was it. No questions asked. Goodbye to the night's sleep. Sit up and work.

This became a kind of routine for months on end. I kept writing, and he kept tearing my attempts up.

***

I once met Dr Harris, professor of English at Mahatma Gandhi University, Kottayam, one of Ayyappa Paniker's favourite students, who had been invited to give a lecture at the institute. He seemed quite interested in my area of research, and one positive bit of advice he gave me was that it would take exactly six months to "get used to AP's ways," and then one would begin to enjoy the torture! (*Ayyappa Paniker Forever*, Folio, 2019: 189–90).

Dhanya went on to complete her research work within the scheduled timeframe, and came to be known as one of Ayyappa Paniker's finest students.

Nisha Venugopal who worked under him for her doctoral degree recalls what Ayyappa Paniker told her when she began her research. She was expected to work for at least 18 hours a day. Dr Roshan Thomas in her tribute to Ayyappa Paniker says, "He taught us to be systematic and methodical and that learning is a lifelong process of the search for perfection. He laid stress on clarity and intelligibility in writing" (*Ayyappa Paniker Forever*, Folio, 2019: 168).

What Ayyappa Paniker wrote about the unique methods of the great scholar Dr K.M. George—who guided young writers inducted into his projects on linguistic and literary exegeses—describes his own modus operandi more aptly:

Dr K.M. George's continuous dedication is surely unparalleled. Most people will experience boredom. And realizing fully that they will feel slightly frustrated, the motivation and the insistence grow stronger. A writer is made to go beyond his ability. I have heard many admit, with happiness and gratification, "I'm tired of Dr George. He won't stop until he breaks me. What a terrible taskmaster!" (*Vyakti Chitrangal, Yatra Drishyangal (Personal Profiles, Travel Sights)*, Cultural Publications Department, Government of Kerala, 2005: 69).

Most research scholars describe him as severe. A majority of those who earned their doctoral degrees under his supervision were women. Discipline, obedience, patience and the ability to focus on a subject intensely for a long time—these qualities are inherent in women. It is also true that a taskmaster can acknowledge or even accept only those who are capable of showing constant enthusiasm and doing hard work. During the time of their research, Ayyappa Paniker, like fathers and mothers of old, was miserly in complimenting them. Occasionally they may have whimpered. But they never withered.

In this context, I remember many of his other bright research scholars like K. Govindan Nair, P.K. Rajan, V.S. Harris, Murali S. and K. Krishnakumar. There were many brave women too who have shared, with great happiness and gratitude, their accounts of the trials they endured as they ascended "the Hill Difficulty" in the course of their research journey. They not only reached respectable positions in their professional lives but also became very ardent admirers of Ayyappa Paniker.

In matters concerning commitment and total surrender to work, presence of mind required for disciplined dedication, obstinate insistence on quality and enthusiasm for patiently working towards the set goal, Ayyappa Paniker would settle for nothing except one hundred per cent. Even 99 per cent fell far short of his expectations. One had to have at least a few of these qualities in order to get close to him. It is an indisputable fact that bright and talented persons were given top priority. But possession of any one or more of the above-mentioned virtues made it possible to have a continued relationship with him.

Research scholars and their families were the chief beneficiaries as well as victims of Ayyappa Paniker's value-based, high-quality lifestyle. Everyone is interested in and zealous about writing on, advocating and listening to the necessity of living such a noble life. Listening to the life stories of such exemplary persons is delightful and they are easy to appreciate too. But how many of those, who have lived with them or spent a lot of time in their company, have assured us that their experiences were thoroughly enjoyable? Did the close associates of Gandhiji, whose great virtues we have read about and still preserve in our memory, find it easy to live and work with him? Maybe such questions do not have much relevance today ...

8
Lankesh Patrike

ON THE DAY of the release of *Sankramanam* in October 1980, possibly on Ayyappa Paniker's request, writer-director-editor P. Lankesh[1] took us to see the printing press of *Lankesh Patrike*. It was a weekly tabloid that was considered to be the mouthpiece of the marginalised. (Later, Gowri Lankesh, his daughter, would take over as its editor and become a tragic victim of the intolerance of Hindutva extremists.) Lankesh was a writer who initiated several revolutionary changes in the social and cultural spheres in Karnataka. He managed all the work related to *Lankesh Patrike*—typesetting, proofreading and editing—before taking the contents to a printing press in a building located close to his house. We observed all the processes

---

1 Palya Lankesh (1935–2000) founded the *Lankesh Patrike* in 1980 and edited it until his death.

in detail. It was not a capital-intensive enterprise and there were no complications or liabilities. It was a relatively simple printing project.

On our way back from Bangalore, Ayyappa Paniker spoke for a long time about the Lankesh model in the printing field and its advantages. He asked me whether I liked it. I replied in the affirmative. I did not realise then that either the release of *Sankramanam* at Bangalore, the long train journey in the company of Ayyappa Paniker or that bit of conversation with him would be turning points in my life.

Let me narrate the subsequent incidents briefly. Barely a month after our return from Bangalore, I took a building on rent, bought the types, and recruited two women employees on a contract basis to do the typesetting work. I planned a system whereby I composed all the matter before I left to attend my classes, and checked the proofs in the evening, after class hours. At night, I took them to the printing press nearby. This became a daily pattern, and it picked up momentum gradually. While I was engaged in *Sankramamam*-related work, I began to receive other remunerative assignments. As a result, before completing my Master's degree in journalism, I managed to purchase a full press and the building. Financial help from my family had made it possible.

Sankramanam then decided to bring out 10 books. The editorial team finalised the titles after discussions with Ayyappa Paniker. At that point, monetary difficulty began to rear its head. Ayyappa Paniker tried to reassure us, saying, "Malayattoor[2] has been drawing illustrations for *Sankramanam*, and is very friendly with you. Don't you know that he's a member of the Advisory Board of the SBT?"[3] But we had heard that the procedures related to loans were endless and wearisome, so we did not have the confidence to proceed with it. Eventually, however, as no alternative appeared in sight and we felt we were losing time, we approached Malayattoor. He told us that Ayyappa Paniker had spoken to him about the problem, and assured us that he would give us whatever help was required. At that point, we wondered why Ayyappa Paniker had never dropped even a hint about it! After engaging us in small talk about literary matters related to *Sankramanam* for some time, Malayattoor instructed us to meet K.T. Rajagopal, the general manager of the SBT. We did that the very next day. Maybe because of Malayattoor's recommendation, the general manager sanctioned us the loan in a week's time. Those were not the days when banks chased their customers and encouraged them to take loans. Despite that, we managed.

In this manner, the Sankramanam book publishing project took off. Under the banner of Sankramanam Pustaka Chakram, 10 books were lined up, including *Kaviyarangu*, Samuel Beckett's *Godoye Kaathu* (*Waiting for Godot*),

---

2 Malayattoor Ramakrishnan, aka K.V. Ramakrishna Iyer (1927–97), bureaucrat-cum-writer and cartoonist, winner of the Kerala Sahitya Akademi Award for Novels and the Vayalar Award. His major works are *Yanthram*, *Verukal*, *Yakshi*, among others.

3 State Bank of Travancore.

U.R. Ananthamurthy's *Avastha*, and titles like *Malayala Cinema* and *Naveena Natakam*. To cut a long story short, the books were published and sold and the loans were repaid as well. Ayyappa Paniker's support was available every step of the way. These books attracted the special attention of readers and critics. With *Kaviyarangu* becoming a prescribed textbook in more than one university, we could pay back the bank loan in time.

Ayyappa Paniker himself selected 60 of his own poems, and translated them into English. The collection, printed at the Sankramanam press, came out as *Selected Poems of Ayyappa Paniker*. I consider it a blessing that we could hand it over to the Modern Book Centre at Thiruvananthapuram for publishing.

I had never imagined that the Sankramanam book publishing venture or its profitable printing press system would become a tangible reality during my academic career. Ayyappa Paniker did not get involved in any of them directly, but he was always by my side as a beacon and sheet anchor.

9
More than an Artist

A PROMINENT WRITER in Malayalam, who worked in a college in Tamil Nadu, fell into dire straits during his last days. When matters became worse and he was severely afflicted with an illness, Ayyappa Paniker stepped in to support him. Besides, he put some of us, who were willing to lend a helping hand, in touch with the person. That was of great relief to the family.

The intervention of Ayyappa Paniker in the life of Dr Sreenath Nair, now an eminent professor at the Lincoln University, became a game-changer. In Sreenath's own words:

> One evening, when the rehearsal of my play *Devashilakal* (Stone Idols) was underway, Paniker sir came to the drama camp along with Ralph Yarrow, his friend and professor of a university in England. Paniker sir's intention was to introduce me to Ralph.

It was a moment that changed my life completely. My friendship with Ralph grew subsequently, and he invited me to do postgraduation at the University of East Anglia in England. Paniker sir himself took the initiative to arrange a small scholarship for me and a loan for higher studies from the State Bank of Travancore. He spoke to Priyadas, showed proof of necessary bank deposits as well as other details of Priyadas's software company, and also a scholarship certificate. What the memories of Ayyappa Paniker leave behind in me is a realisation that there are certain debts in one's life that can never ever be repaid.

Later, Dr Sreenath and his wife Arya became teachers at Lincoln University in England, and continue to teach there to this day.

One of the Class IV employees at the Institute of English used to suffer financial difficulties from time to time. On such occasions, Ayyappa Paniker would help him out, without letting anyone know about it. The beneficiary himself admitted this to P.I. Abraham, the administrative officer at the Institute of English at that time.

The poet Raghavan Atholi[1] once requested Ayyappa Paniker to write a foreword to his collection of poems, and Ayyappa Paniker obliged. Subsequently, this was how he recounted the experience in *Kerala Kavitha*:

---

1 Raghavan Atholi (b. 1957) is a prolific writer, best known for his collection of poems titled *Kandathi*, a novel called *Choraparisham* and so on.

It was not generosity shown by a *savarna* towards a Dalit's poems. But wasn't it generosity itself? Paniker sir took money out of his own pocket in order to get my book published. If that was not generosity, what is?

Paniker sir is my poet-father. A father who gave me a distinct position, voice and style among poets, and made me a poet. To me, he is not Ayyappa Paniker. He is Achappa[2] Paniker (*Kerala Kavitha*, 2007: 186).

The poet and teacher, Deshamangalam Ramakrishnan, testifies that Ayyappa Paniker extended financial support not only to Raghavan Atholi but many other poets as well so that they could get their works published.

Once Ayyappa Paniker asked me whether I could give employment to a young boy named Jayakrishnan in the software firm named Guild Soft which I owned and managed. He said that since Jayakrishnan's family was going through a severe financial crisis, giving him a job would be a great help. I sought the youth's biodata, interviewed and eventually took him in, and he worked in the company for several years. Ayyappa Paniker never held himself back whenever anyone—be it an individual, an institution or even a university—needed any help.

When Dr Radhakrishna Warrier, the director of publications of Mahatma Gandhi University, was working as an assistant editor, he used to write letters to various

---

2 "Father" in Malayalam.

writers seeking permission to include their poems, stories or critical pieces in textbooks that the university was planning to publish. Most of them wanted to know how much remuneration they would get. But Ayyappa Paniker's reply was "Permission granted", followed by his signature. Warrier states that Ayyappa Paniker's responses were always positive. They came in the form of constructive ideas and encouraging instructions, without any thought about returns.

Ayyappa Paniker took special care to ensure no one knew about his largesse. Rendering help, as he saw it, was a matter of duty or responsibility. It was an assignment to be shouldered, a mission to be undertaken. The Christian diktat "Don't let your left hand know what your right hand is doing" was the principle that ruled his life. He was a lighted wick which dispelled darkness.

Whenever I think of him, I am reminded of his words about Victor Hugo: "What we see in Victor Hugo's novels is perhaps more of a philanthropist throbbing with humanism than an artist" (*Vishwa Sahityathiloode* [Through World Literature], Vol. 2, 2006: 87).

10
Modernism is Dead. Long Live Modernism

BY THE EARLY 1980s, modernism surged beyond the confines of its image as a cultural wave, and grew into an indisputably strong literary and cultural movement. That was a period when modernists in the field of arts—poetry, fiction, drama and film—were given awards and feted everywhere. But as it happens in all movements, even as modernism gathered strength, weaknesses began to set in. Certain cliques, which showered praises on one another in the name of modernism, began to sprout during that time.

But through our editorials we repeatedly swore *Sankramanam* was a magazine that fought such regressive tendencies in literature. (We never cudgelled our brains over our own eligibility to make such claims.) We gave prominence to works that criticised those who opposed the political and cultural stances taken by the magazine. Orthodox elements in the field of arts and poets who dismissed non-metrical poetry as mere prose were subjected to criticism. Surely, the harsh editorials, written in the full flush of youthful zeal and immaturity, would have wounded at least a few. But our readers kept on encouraging us.

During those days, when we were engaged in a crusade against the establishment, modernism itself appeared to get transformed into one. Even the behaviour of many writers seemed to be in sync with that spirit. They displayed an air of arrogance, and it appeared as if public acknowledgement of their writings as well as demeanour had gone to their heads! (Maybe it was a mere impression we gathered at that point of time.) Thus, some writers were lauded and others diplomatically devalued in public forums and weeklies by certain cliques. Many members of such cliques were contributors of articles in *Sankramanam*, and they had loyal followers among the readers.

However, as part of a firm commitment to the ideals we held aloft, many issues of *Sankramanam* carried pieces that were critical of these writers. If anyone were to ask us today, "How could you attack writers who had cooperated with *Sankramanam*?" we would have no satisfactory answers to give.

Four litterateurs who had been sharply criticised in the pages of *Sankramanam* decided to band themselves together, and stop this aggressive style of journalism we had adopted. They met Ayyappa Paniker at the Institute of English and presented a resolution against the magazine, especially against its editor. They told Ayyappa Paniker that as he did not interfere in whatever got published in *Sankramanam*, the editor was using the sword of independence to slash them. So, their request was that Ayyappa Paniker should withdraw the unconditional support he extended to the magazine. They argued their case in front of him, arraying a few copies of *Sankramanam* as proof.

Later, they themselves spoke of this meeting with Ayyappa Paniker to a few of their friends, and the news reached me in due course. Although I had not done anything seriously wrong, stress began to froth continuously in my mind as I prepared myself for an interface with Ayyappa Paniker. I worried about his reaction, but he never spoke to me about the meeting the four writers had had with him and I did not see any perceptible difference in his attitude towards me.

I published the next issue with the headline "Modernism is Dead. Long Live Modernism". As was customary, we picked up a copy of the issue, and took it to Ayyappa Paniker. We felt this was an opportunity for him to respond to the accusations made against us by those writers. Although he had not uttered a word previously, that did not matter. But this issue was conspicuously about the specific subject. So, any slight shift in his mood or opinion was of crucial importance. I tried my best not to let any of my stress show. Ayyappa Paniker read M.K. Sanoo's article on the cover page, that could be construed as a reply to the accusations made by those writers and said approvingly, "Very good!" M.K. Sanoo's arguments were exclusively about the fissures that had appeared within modernism because of the excessive acknowledgement it had received.

The portrait of the great *guru*—who without uttering a word conveyed a profound message of standing by what was right, by disregarding organised power and refusing to buckle under pressure—continues to be my guiding light, and glows in my mind. In course of time, Ayyappa Paniker was witness to these very same writers becoming my personal friends and well-wishers of *Sankramanam*. And to this day, I am not sure whether he had a role to play in it.

11
Strange Tastes

IN 1980, A few days after the demise of Jean-Paul Sartre, Ayyappa Paniker suddenly flung a question at us: "What do you have in the Sartre special issue of *Sankramanam*?" As we had not had such a thought at all, we were utterly flummoxed and flooded with guilt. After all, in the previous years we had discussed existentialism and the writers whose works reflected the philosophy. And yet, we had not thought about a special issue after hearing that Sartre had passed away! That was how we began to consider the idea seriously.

It seemed simple at first but on deeper contemplation, the project looked challenging. Eventually, we started work on the special publication. Later, it would be evaluated as the best issue of *Sankramanam*, which was not surprising, considering the galaxy of writers who contributed articles for it—Narendra Prasad, K.P. Appan, Asha Menon, V. Rajakrishnan,

G. Aravindan, M. Gangadharan, M. Mukundan, Aliyar, D. Vinayachandran and Ayyappa Paniker.

In 1982, when Lebanon was attacked, Kuripuzha Sreekumar, the poet, who was disturbed by the developments, wrote a poem on the subject. (He was a very popular young poet then, famous for his poetic performances as well as his stances.) But he tore the paper to bits. In a couple of days, Ayyappa Paniker wrote a poem titled "Lebanon", which *Sankramanam* carried.

> Lebanon,
> who exhales hot breath from among the cedar trees!
> Do not forgive us,
> who shot weapons against you
> in your helpless moment!
> Do not crumble on seeing our silence
> when the tragic stage of human story, rendered rootless,
> collapses.

On reading it, Kuripuzha Sreekumar's response was: "In reality, Ayyappa Paniker's poetry was a challenge to youthful poetic voices. By the time the youth firmed up their poetic thought, Ayyappa Paniker would already have written about it" (*Ayyappa Paniker: Jeevitharekha* [*Ayyappa Paniker: Life Sketch*], DC Books, 2007: 85). In his own special way, Ayyappa Paniker used to challenge many people in order to draw out their hidden talents. It was a call that aroused the dormant voice within. A few recognised that as the suggestion was rendered in a gentle manner, no one perceived it as a challenge. Some of the questions sounded like harmless instructions or opinions, aired casually and in passing. Certain others were admittedly provocative, though without a tone of defiance or any emotion accompanying it.

Young poets were not the only ones whom Ayyappa Paniker challenged. He kept on taunting those who approached closer, taking into consideration the special talents and behavioural traits of each. What Ayyappa Paniker did in one way or another was to trigger a determination in them. Bharat Murali[1] remembers, "It was the occasion of the death anniversary of C.N. (C.N. Sreekantan Nair).[2] He [Ayyappa Paniker] asked me whether I would play the role of Ravana in *Lanka Lakshmi*. As I could not refuse him anything, I consented at that moment. But when I thought more about the performance, I was dumbfounded. If I could not take up a challenge, why act at all? I had given my word to Paniker sir. I could not go back on it" (*Kerala Kavitha*, 2007: 189).

After the play was staged, Ayyappa Paniker and many other stalwarts in the field of drama, who were among the audience, congratulated Murali most heartily. The words he used to provoke gentle, ordinary people were less severe ones.

When four poems from Ayyappa Paniker's *Pathumanippookkal* ("Poetry at Midnight") were translated

---

1 Bharat Murali (1954–2009) was a highly accomplished and celebrated theatre personality, film actor and author.

2 C.N. Sreekantan Nair (1928–76) was a playwright and screenplay writer who authored plays like *Kanchana Sita*, *Lanka Lakshmi*, *Saketam* and so on.

by P. Ravindran Nayar, the south Indian bureau chief of the United News of India (UNI), and published in *The New Indian Express*, Ayyappa Paniker asked Nayar casually, "In that case, why not do the rest as well?" The task sounded easy but when he set out to do it in all seriousness, the translator realised the project he had undertaken presented a great deal of difficulty. Sometimes, when he called Ayyappa Paniker to cross-check the intended meanings of certain words or lines, Paniker kept away from any kind of intervention, stating that translation was a creative process. After the translation work got completed, Ayyappa Paniker read the full text. When Ravindran Nayar saw a hearty smile blossoming on the poet's face, he thanked Paniker for having given him the opportunity, and touched his feet in reverence.

Once, Kavalam Anand, Ayyappa Paniker's sister's son, after taking his Master's degree in English literature from University College, Thiruvananthapuram, was toying with the idea of contacting and doing research on the author, Mulk Raj Anand. Ayyappa Paniker, who had heard that Mulk Raj Anand was scheduled to attend a Sahitya Akademi function at Ernakulam, called his nephew over phone and conveyed the information. When Anand asked him where the author would be staying, Ayyappa Paniker's response was, "Go to Ernakulam and find out!" I recall Anand admitting that it took him considerable time to realise the first lesson of research—only hard work yielded results—had been imparted to him.

Aliyar V. Kunju, the academic and famous Malayalam artist, who translated many Kannada works including Girish

Karnad's *Tughlaq* into Malayalam, conceded that, "It was Paniker sir who asked for translations of most of them. Every time we met, he gave me one task or another. He would suggest a topic and ask me to attempt an article, or translate a poem or a play."

P.K. Balakrishnan, the writer, recalling the days he spent writing a critical work titled *Novel: Siddhiyum Saadhanayum* (published in 1964), admitted:

> During those two years, he was of help to me at various levels (and it was consciously done). Most of the books came from his own collection. It was this same friend who recommended many titles that were unfamiliar to me. Almost on a daily basis, he showed interest in the progress of my work, and made me aware of his sincere anxiety to see the work executed well. I think, during the most difficult phases of writing, I continued to write, keeping in mind this man's strange interest, and aiming to earn that recognition (*Novel: Siddhiyum Saadhanayum*, DC Books, 2006: 11).

In fact, in most cases, many individuals were astonished at their own ability to overcome challenges and scale great heights, solely because they were powered by a desire to fulfil Ayyappa Paniker's expectations even when they seemed to cross all reasonable limits.

12
Enemy/Friend

THAYAT SANKARAN, THE editor of *Deshabhimani*, a weekly Malayalam newspaper, wrote a book titled *Adhunika Kavithayude Jeerna Mukham* (The Decayed Face of Modernist Poetry) in which he criticised Ayyappa Paniker's poetry.

In response to the arguments he had made in it, Renji Panicker wrote an article titled "*Ee Jeernicha Mukham Adhunika Kavithayudeyo Marxian Nirupanathinteyo*" (This Decayed Face is that of Modernist Poetry or Marxian Criticism?). It was given due prominence, and presented as a cover page story in the November 1983 issue of *Sankramanam*. Even before the ink on it went dry, Renji Panicker and I dashed to Ayyappa Paniker's house to gather all the praise we were sure he would shower on us. Ayyappa Paniker looked at the cover page, and slowly went into the inner pages to read the rest of the contents. Our eyes widened in sheer pride.

However, to our consternation, Ayyappa Paniker did not compliment or praise us. Instead, he told us that critics should not be viewed as enemies. They were our true friends who corrected us and helped us grow. Therefore, there was no need to oppose anyone. He added that, like critics, there were aesthetes too who had the ability to evaluate poems and make their own assessment. At that age, we could not fully understand or assimilate what he said, and we returned to our circle of friends to celebrate the occasion.

During that time, there was a rumour that O.N.V. Kurup and Ayyappa Paniker were enemies. At the very least, they occupied opposite ends of the poetic spectrum. So, people could not be faulted if they imagined that the two poets were at loggerheads with each other in life too. Both were teachers—O.N.V. taught Malayalam, while Ayyappa Paniker specialised in English. They were of nearly the same age but followed two entirely different poetic paths. O.N.V. had been involved with the Kerala People's Arts Club (KPAC)[1] and evolved along with it. Later, he contested the general elections as a left candidate. Ayyappa Paniker, on the other hand, was a figure in the cultural arena who showed no allegiance towards any movement. Besides, he was very firm about not lending his poetic skills to the field of Malayalam playback music. O.N.V., however, saw nothing wrong in composing lyrics for Malayalam films to suit the situations picturised in

---

1 The KPAC, a theatrical movement formed in 1950, played a very crucial role in popularizing communism in Kerala, and bringing about a radical change in the cultural and political scenes in the state.

them. Both rarely shared a public forum together. But when Ayyappa Paniker heard about O.N.V.'s ill health, he rushed to the latter's side. This is testified by Dr M.M. Basheer who was a close friend of both families.

At a time when *Kerala Kavitha* was deeply involved in popularizing modernist poetry, Ayyappa Paniker had to leave for the US to do his doctoral research at Indiana University. What he did before leaving left everyone stunned. He put O.N.V. in charge of its editorial responsibilities! O.N.V. wrote about it like this:

> I understand from my experiences that Ayyappa Paniker's approach was to respect every poet's creative freedom. That was the reason he felt confident about asking me to shoulder the editorial responsibility of *Kerala Kavitha* despite the fact that I followed a poetic path that was utterly different from his. How could people travelling in opposite directions be friends? Even a few of our friends had such misgivings (*Kerala Kavitha*, 2007: 104).

Ayyappa Paniker took such a decision at a time when he was the helmsman of modernist poetry, and the older generation of the literary world was still hesitant about acknowledging his presence. He was merely 38 years old then. It is only natural for humans to become wise with age, but the self-confidence and maturity Ayyappa Paniker showed in handing over the editorial reins when he was in the prime of his life reveal the philosophical approach and perspective he had towards life. That was a period when Ayyappa Paniker gained attention in the literary field as a gentle rebel who took strong stances as he moved forward. Ayyappa Paniker knew that getting recognition for one's views and gaining respectability came only by giving adequate space to those who had opposing outlooks.

Many of us may not be able to accommodate those whose thought processes, poetic methods and lifestyles are contrary to ours, let alone respect them or maintain them as friends. But Ayyappa Paniker saw nothing unnatural about it. Dr P.V. Velayudhan Pillai, head of the Department of Malayalam at the University of Kerala, recalled:

> Once I wrote an article in *Granthalokam* that was not very complimentary about Paniker's poetry. The title of the article was "Rajavu Mundu Uduthittilla".[2] *Granthalokam* hit the market stands. That very evening, Ayyappa Paniker and I happened to meet at Statue junction. We greeted each other and made small talk. Then Paniker said, "Today, I'm wearing a *mundu*". I laughed, understanding his implication fully well. Paniker, who used to wear pants occasionally, was in a *mundu* that day. That was the end of the conversation. His face radiated the customary joyful smile. The number of times we met later! The number of projects we did! Even today, we are friends who understand each other (*Ayyappa Paniker: Vyakthiyum Kaviyum* [Ayyappa Paniker: The Individual and the Poet], DC Books, 1990: 42).

---

2 A Malayalam variant of "The Emperor Has No Clothes". Here, *mundu* refers to a *dhoti*, an unstitched cloth worn (usually) by Malayali men at the waist and reaching up to the ankles.

Dr Velayudhan Pillai cites several other instances that show how any difference of opinion in Ayyappa Paniker's eyes was no obstacle to continued friendship or a factor that led to enmity.

Atmaraman (Krishna Kumar) the poet, critic and formerly student at the Institute of English, in his account of Ayyappa Paniker, noted that Paniker gave due respect, sometimes more than was warranted, to those who criticised him from an opposite camp. It did not matter how young the critics were or how low their status was.

> I have expressed my disaffection with his poetry on more than one occasion, directly and publicly. But when I recall how despite it, he never showed any lack of interest in me, I tear up. More significantly, he constantly encouraged me to keep writing. I do not know many poets who maintain friendship with those who find fault with their poetry (*Bhashaposhini*, 2006 October: 34).

When someone defies the prevailing notions about art, culture and life, and becomes an advocate of an alternative model, it is only natural to have enemies. But Ayyappa Paniker opposed ideas, not individuals. Small minds waste their time criticizing individuals—but great minds discuss ideas. Ayyappa Paniker subscribed to that philosophy.

He quarrelled not with tradition but with the undesirable tendencies within it. Ayyappa Paniker must have decided that he did not require, nor did it suit his nature, to earn fame or attract the attention of the press by criticizing poets by citing their names. In an article titled "T. S. Eliot", that was published in *The Democrat* in 1950, he argued that metre and other traditional parameters were not the hallmarks of great poetry—he made his point gently but firmly, without mentioning any poem or naming any poet, and conveyed his criticism through poetry and humour. I feel that if he had enemies either in the literary field or in his workplace, it may have been because they could not understand him. The fact is that he did not see anyone as his enemy.

What was Ayyappa Paniker's attitude towards those who fell out with him? How was his behaviour towards them? In the course of my investigation in this direction, I decided to contact his daughter Meena and ask my questions directly. As we were in frequent touch with each other, there was no need for any formality. So, I asked her openly, "Did Ayyappa Paniker have any enemies?"

"Yes ..."

Taken aback, I became silent for a moment. Then I persisted, "Who were they?"

Meena quoted the first line from her father's "*Shatrubhayam*" ("Fear of the Enemy"): "I had an enemy called Ayyappa Paniker" (*Selected Poems of Ayyappa Paniker*, Trivandrum, Modern Book Centre, 1985: 101).

> During all the years of my association with him, I never saw him snap at, scold or get angry with anyone. Even if anyone went up to him in order to pick a quarrel, they had to return disappointed. He slipped away like

a small cake of soap. With extraordinary smartness and cunning, he invariably twisted a word used by the opponent, and made the scene light (*Ayyappa Paniker: Vyakthiyum Kaviyum* [Ayyappa Paniker: The Individual and the Poet], DC Books, 1990: 52).

Ayyappa Paniker's poems like "*Shatrumithram*" ("Enemy/Friend"), "*Thekkum Vadakkum*" ("South and North") and "180°" suggest that what we consider as oppositional entities are really not so, and what we see as contradictions are in reality complementary ideas.

The enemy is actually a friend and vice versa. And aren't north and south hypothetical concepts, after all?

C.J. said:
   Beware of enemies. Also friends.

Quoth Govindan:
   Take care of enemies, otherwise they
   Turn into friends. Friends will
   Take care of us.

Sukumar spake:
   The opposite.
   Friends will
   Turn into enemies
   Whether you care or not.

Srikantan responded:
   In case we do not care,
   That phenomenon may naturally manifest.

I asked:
> Who is the friend? Who the enemy?

Ramakrishnan caught on:
> The enemy of the friend is the friend of the enemy.

Balan hymned:
> The friend is the enemy, The enemy the friend.
> Let us go (Days *and Nights*, the National Educational Research Centre [NERC], 2001: 97).

13
Invisible Power

AFTER THE INDEPENDENCE struggle, the 1970s and the '80s were the decades which witnessed the most intense cultural quakes and vibrations in Kerala. The tremors in the fields of arts, poetry, theatre, cinema and politics impacted the Malayali consciousness, even unconsciously. This infused a vibrancy in all facets of culture. Anyone who stepped into youth during that time would have found it difficult to miss the aura of Ayyappa Paniker's presence.

It was highly unlikely for the youth of that time to escape participation in any one of the cultural activities either conducted or managed by Ayyappa Paniker. He introduced many famous and yet-to-be-famous artists of the cultural field of that period to the aesthetes of Kerala. In the evenings, he went to the drama rehearsals conducted by Kavalam Narayana Panicker or Narendra Prasad. And there are many who can testify to the claim made by Kavalam (in the book *Ayyappa Paniker: Vyakthiyum Kaviyum* [Ayyappa Paniker: The Individual and the Poet]), that Ayyappa Paniker was the epicentre of the quakes that aroused the cultural minds of Malayalis from the 1970s.

The poetic performances and recitals that Ayyappa Paniker and his circle of poet-friends organised from the first half of the 1970s, raised the level of communication between the creator and the spectator to greater heights. When the poet's compositions took on the voices, the rhythms and the emotions of the reciters, they imparted utterly new auditory and visual experiences to the aesthetes. The dramatic presentations of poems on stage made the works very popular and poetic images were converted into spectacles. All this was conducted under the spiritual guidance of Ayyappa Paniker.

Along with the poets, notable theatre personalities like Kodiyettam Gopi, Murali (Muraleedharan Pillai), Nedumudi Venu, Jagannathan, Aliyar, M.K. Gopalakrishnan and M.V. Gopakumar participated in the performances. Ayyappa Paniker's invisible leadership and participation was perceived in the establishment and growth of various drama institutions like G. Sankara Pillai's *"Nataka Kalari"*, Kavalam Narayana Panicker's indigenous theatre named *"Sopanam"*, Kochunarayanan's *"Ranga Prabhath"* and Narendra Prasad's *"Natya Griham"*. He stood as a strong source of support to playwrights like C.J. Thomas, C.N. Sreekantan Nair, Kavalam Narayana Panicker, G. Sankara Pillai, Narendra Prasad and others. Narayana Panicker has stated that Ayyappa Paniker who had a deep interest in all aspects of the dramatic culture that was popularly known as "indigenous theatre"—right from the rehearsal to the final stage presentation—was a playwright who had not composed a play (*Ayyappa Paniker: Vyakthiyum Kaviyum* [Ayyappa Paniker: The Individual and the Poet], DC Books, 1990: 70).

Through his presence, closeness and participation in conversations, Ayyappa Paniker provided inspiration and support to artistes for whom Kathakali, Koodiyattam, Nangyarkoothu, Chakyarkoothu, Kalaripayattu and folk arts were the breath of life. He encouraged Appukuttan Nair to establish "Margi," a Kathakali school, and helped him run it successfully. Artists like M.V. Devan, Kanayi Kunhiraman, Paris Vishwanathan, B.D. Dathan, Narayana Bhattathiri, Rajendran, Lizzie Jacob and others basked under his aura of inspiration and love.

In the special issue of the *Sankramanam* dedicated to the visual arts in 1984, Ayyappa Paniker wrote an article titled "The Three Pioneers of Malayalam Cinema" in which he made an objective evaluation of three directors. Analysing their creative courage and their films, he described them as the creators and propagators of a new sensibility. And the comment he made in the context—"Good cinema is the life-blood of a creative director"—had a tremendous impact because the confidence it imparted to the upcoming generations of the proponents of New Cinema was not insignificant. He gave support to all who showed the courage to walk the untrodden paths of cinema, including people like K.P. Kumaran, Pavithran, T.V. Chandran and others.

In 1989, after viewing Shaji N. Karun's film *Piravi*, Ayyappa Paniker wrote: "Each frame of *Piravi* is a testimony to the fact that Shaji and his colleagues are committed minds."

Most people are interested in being in the foreground because it guarantees them name and fame. But Ayyappa Paniker was not interested in anything of that kind. He believed that his place was not on the stage but either behind it or among the audience. Neither his physique, demeanour, conversational style, body language, gait nor behavioural traits pandered to the common perceptions or expectations of a leader who stood out in a crowd. For him, this was a convenience rather than a concern. Precisely for that reason, though he was extraordinary, he experienced no difficulty in leading the life of an ordinary man. He rewrote popular notions about the image of a leader. In short, he was a colossus who towered above positions of power and tokens of recognition.

14
Humour in Conversation

AFTER AYYAPPA PANIKER'S 90th birth anniversary celebrations got over, I gave serious thought to starting a YouTube programme along with Nedumudi Venu who was very close to Ayyappa Paniker. My idea was to have Nedumudi Venu share Ayyappa Paniker's jokes with the public, in a conversational style. Venu promised to sit down and discuss the details with me as soon as his film shooting schedules got over. When I heard that he had a huge stock of Ayyappa Paniker's jokes, I was more elated. But while I was in the thick of making preparations for the project, Venu was hospitalised, and he passed away soon thereafter. Now, I recall some of the jokes he shared with me.

***

After the play *Deivathar* (although impossible to translate easily, generally speaking, the word means "god", that is, specifically the god worshipped in the Malabar region of north Kerala) was presented on stage, several spectators went to the green room to meet the actors. One of them wanted to meet the drummer—his name was Padmanabhan but he was more popularly known as Mon Kuttan. Ayyappa Paniker pointed out Mon Kuttan to the admirer and said, "There! That is Mon Kottan!"[1]

***

Once when the actor and screenwriter Nedumudi Venu returned home, his wife informed him that Ayyappa Paniker had telephoned a couple of times. He had left word that Nedumudi Venu should return the call as soon as he got back. Why did Ayyappa Paniker, who called only during times of utmost necessity, telephone him several times? Nedumudi Venu was perturbed. He rang up Ayyappa Paniker and said, "I was told you called many times, sir."

"Yes, I did."

"What is it about, sir?"

"Such matters need not fall on wives' ears, you see. It may cause family discord."

Venu became more troubled but he managed to ask, "What crime did I commit, sir?"

"Oh! It's nothing, really. Only about your taking a membership of the C.V. Foundation. One thousand rupees.

---

[1] *Kuttan* in Malayalam means "little (male) child". *Kottan* means "drummer".

In such matters, most people within our circle do things without their wives' knowledge …"

***

Another day, Ayyappa Paniker telephoned Nedumudi Venu. Although Venu could identify his voice, it was unclear and sounded as if coming from afar. "I can't hear you, sir," Venu said. Immediately, there was the sound of something being rectified at the other end.

"How's it now?"

"No, sir. It is still not clear."

Another series of sounds followed.

"Now, do you hear me?" Ayyappa Paniker asked.

"Yes, sir. I can."

"Finally! There's at least one person in Thiruvananthapuram who'll hear me out!" came Ayyappa Paniker's repartee.

***

Nedumudi Venu wrote about Ayyappa Paniker thus, "There is a cheerful, mischievous boy accompanying Ayyappa Paniker sir all the time. The boy does not miss a single opportunity to play games. It's like the Golden Cassia admitting 'I can't help blossoming'.[2] He does not present any subject in a way we are accustomed to hearing it, either in

---

2 The reference is to Ayyappa Paniker's own poem "*Pookaathirikkaan Enikkaavathille*".

his writing or in his speech" (*Samakalika Malayalam*, 2000 September: 40).

Humour is meant to evoke laughter, and the easiest way to make people laugh is by making fun of someone. But Ayyappa Paniker's humour came more from harmless teasing than having a dig at someone—and he invariably conveyed a profound message through it. There were not many in Ayyappa Paniker's generation, other than Vaikom Muhammad Basheer, V.K.N. (Vadakkke Koottala Narayanankutty Nair) or a few other prose writers, who handled humour adeptly in their day-to-day as well as their creative life.

Ayyappa Paniker was not merely humourous, but that does not mean he did not crack light jokes. Most of them went beyond evoking mere laughter. They can be categorised into three: laugh-evoking jokes (in conversations), laugh- and thought-provoking jokes (in prose writings) and laugh- and thought-provoking and rejuvenating jokes (in poetry in the form of irony). They are also classified as harmless jokes, satirical jokes and pure or well-intentioned jokes. The Ayyappa Paniker jokes compiled by Dr Raju Vallikkunnu and published by DC Books is titled *Ayyappa Panikerude Narmasambhashanangalum Narmakavithakalum* (Ayyappa Paniker's Humorous Conversations and Humorous Poetry).

All the jokes that he cracked were appropriate to the context. For instance, once Ayyappa Paniker and a few friends were sitting in a small room awaiting Kadammanitta. The latter finally came, an umbrella tucked under his armpit.

As he stepped in, the umbrella preceded him. Immediately, Ayyappa Paniker remarked, "Here comes Kudammanitta!"[3]

***

Even compliments fell from Ayyappa Paniker's lips in the form of jokes. Aliyar was out of station and could not attend C.N. Sreekantan Nair's play *Lanka Lakshmi* in which Murali had put up a sterling performance, playing various roles without any change in make-up or costume. The next day, he went to Ayyappa Paniker, and asked him about Murali's acting.

"Splendid! It was splendid. But what can we do? We can't do a thing about it!"

***

Most of the time, Ayyappa Paniker made corrections through humour. Once he was invited to the retirement function of Aliyar who had served as the head of the Department of Malayalam at University College in Thiruvananthapuram. The other invitee was Ganesh Kumar, the state minister for transport.

While Aliyar was a teacher at the Arts' College, Ganesh Kumar had been his student. But an organiser, who was not aware of this connection, enquired whether it would not be better to invite the minister for education or culture for the function. Ayyappa Paniker quelled the doubt by replying, "Isn't this a send-off function? There can't be a more suitable guest than the transport minister," amidst peals of laughter.

---

3 *Kuda* in Malayalam means "umbrella".

He continued, "Aliyar arrived [into collegiate service] thirty years back. Now he is departing. All the more reason why the transport minister should grace the occasion."[4]

***

As with "Mon Kuttan", playing with names was Ayyappa Paniker's forte. Once when he arrived at a drama camp, he enquired who the camp director was. Aliyar replied it was S. Ramanujam, the doyen of Tamil theatre and a close friend of Ayyappa Paniker's. "Oh! Our very own Dramanujam!" Ayyappa Paniker quipped.

***

Language was never an obstacle in Ayyappa Paniker's path. Both Malayalam and English yielded themselves to his humorous tongue.

One day, Ayyappa Paniker was accompanying a group of Russian guests to a theatre for a dramatic presentation. Kavalam's son Hari was behind the wheel. As the play was about to begin, Hari drove the car really fast. The foreigners were scared and looked at Ayyappa Paniker anxiously. But he consoled them, "Don't worry. His name is 'Hurry'!"

***

Once, in 1977, Prabhakar Machwe, the central minister, was invited to inaugurate the first World Malayali Conference. As the work on the pavilion was

---

[4] Instance of a brilliant play of words here. The Malayalam word for "arrival" is *aagatham* and "departure" is *gatham*. The word for "transport" is *gathaagatham*.

still underway, the minister stopped at a point and asked, "Which way?"

"Much way!" came Ayyappa Paniker's response to Machwe.

***

Once when Ayyappa Paniker arrived in Mumbai to attend a literary meeting, a local poet asked him, "Did you come all the way from Thiruvananthapuram?"

Ayyappa Paniker's reply was, "Yes, because I had no other way."

***

Instances of such an ingenious play with words peppered his conversations throughout his life. Each was triggered on the spur of the moment. Although they were never the result of deliberation, the jokes left much room for thought. Ayyappa Paniker's humour leavened his conversations and his works in numerous ways, accompanying him naturally wherever he travelled. Whether a person was known to him or not, it was not possible for anyone to leave his company without experiencing his humour at some level or another.

15
Humour in Poetry

ONCE, THE KERALA University Departments' Union decided to set apart an entire afternoon of a poets' meet for the benefit of students. All the major poets were invited to the function. Arrangements for picking them from various parts of the city, and organising the meet were finally over. But, due to some reason, classes scheduled for that particular afternoon were suspended and many students left the campus, the information of this reaching us only in the afternoon. However, we thought that since students generally liked poets' meets and other cultural programmes, the function would go smoothly. But there were many empty seats in the hall.

Suddenly, those of us who were members of the organising committee had a brainwave. We could import many students from the hostels! Immediately we rushed on our bikes and any other small vehicles we could lay our hands on, and collected several hostel inmates to fill the seats. It did not matter much that some of them were not in formal wear. To cut a long story short, we managed to have a full audience before the invited poets entered the hall. And our mood was upbeat.

The poets' meet began well. Sugathakumari teacher rendered her poem "*Krishna nee enne ariyilla ...*" ("Krishna, you don't know me ..."). The next poet was Ayyappa Paniker. When he recited the first line of his poem *Gopikadandakam* ("The Song of the Cowherdess"): *Ariyunnuninnenjaangopike* ... (I do understand you, O cowherdess ...), as though in reply to the plaintive notes of the earlier poem, the crowd was jolted out of the sorrowful ambience. And by the time Ayyappa Paniker started to recite a couple of his cartoon poems, the crowd began to keep the time.

By 4 p.m., the poets' meet came to a close. The organisers and the audience were happy. I jumped into the car that was slated to take Ayyappa Paniker back home. During our conversation in the car, I remarked that a lot of students liked poetry, and that many of them had an interest in creative writing too. Then I went a step further to claim that whenever poets' meets were arranged, we were sure of a packed hall. At this point, Ayyappa Paniker asked, "The students in the campus attend classes wearing *lungi*s,[1] don't they?"

---

1 Coloured and/or patterned *dhoti*s, usually worn by adult men as home wear.

I realised that Ayyappa Paniker had seen the casually dressed youths, and understood the truth about our rounding up students from hostels to fill up all the vacant seats. Utterly embarrassed, I remained silent and looked at him piteously. His mischievous smile only deepened my sense of shame. Inwardly, I told myself, "Just because I have stolen a few things, why should you call me a thief?"[2] Maybe Ayyappa Paniker understood my predicament. He quickly channelled the conversation to other matters.

Ayyappa Paniker may possibly be one of the writers who has composed the most number of humourous poems in Malayalam. Through him, Malayalis have been exposed to many shades of humour like self-mockery, satire, paradoxical humour, pure jokes, black humour and so on. His black poems, paradoxes, cartoon poems, maharaja tales and satires are famous. Two versions of "*Moshanam*" ("Theft")— one rendered in the style of indigenous folk poetry by Nedumudi Venu, Kavalam Sreekumar and their group, and the other performed in the Western style and directed by K.D. Shybu Mundakkal—are very popular among YouTube viewers.

The cartoon poems were humourous pieces written during the time of the Emergency. In the poem "*Phalithan*" ("Humourist"), Ayyappa Paniker wrote:

---

[2] The reference is to one of Ayyappa Paniker's most famous poems, titled "*Moshanam*" ("Theft") (*Days and Nights*, NERC: 116).

> In the national political circus
> He donned the role of a clown.

"Kaala Vishesham" ("News of the Hour"):

> If I had had a thousand gold sovereigns,
> I would have grown into a leader.
> If my tongue had been four miles long,
> I would have become a scholar.

"Poura Bodham" ("Civic Sense"):

> Why a road in front of our house
> If not to throw our rubbish on?
> Why a national highway stretching its back all along the land
> If not for Ittunni to conduct processions and halt traffic?

"Njan Oru Tyagi" ("I am a Self-sacrificing Person"):

> I am a self-sacrificing person
> Love of humankind, a weakness of mine.
> When I can't sacrifice something
> On certain occasions, that is another sacrifice.
> I am a self-sacrificing person.

"Kimvadanthi" ("Hearsay"):

> Long ago roamed in the forest shade
> A man who herded goats

Seeing his long beard, another sang:
"That's Ramana[3] Maharshi!"

"*Himalayan*":

> I don't have great love
> For Himalayan, you know!
> Reason: firstly, the height.
> It doesn't suit our land.
> ... ...
> If it's razed down to the coast level
> I can reconsider. But only if you feel like.
> There's no compulsion.

"*Kuthira*" ("Horse"):

> Seeing a bike on the road,
> A horse told its donkey-mother:
> Mother, I cannot gallop like this.
> You must buy me a bike
> So that I can glide over the road like that.

What Ayyappa Paniker did through his poetry was to evoke humour. As he did not address those who sat in front of him but rather spoke to those in a future time and space, the humour in his poetry assumed a different

---

3 The reference is to the eponymous, famous cowherd-hero in Changampuzha Krishna Pillai's famous pastoral elegy "*Ramanan*". "Ramana Maharshi," however, is an entirely different person – a spiritual leader popularly known as the Sage of Arunachala.

dimension. His poems were rooted in the power of suggestions and hints. They contained paradoxes that triggered not an immediate burst of laughter but carried potential for thought-provoking enjoyment. These poems, therefore, led the readers to the opposite meaning. Irony, in his hands, was not a mere technique. It had philosophical dimensions too.

I have always felt that Ayyappa Paniker saw life itself as an irony. Perhaps that was why, like in Soren Kierkegaard's quotes, there was a dichotomy in Ayyappa Paniker's take on life. Such people remain present in all states of life, participate in it, and even get completely involved sometimes. But they do all this, while maintaining a kind of spiritual distance. Their mental state accommodates a combination of neutrality and commitment; or indifference and dedication. Ayyappa Paniker's mind reflected the complementarity of these dichotomous states and the spiritual poise that emerged from it.

16
Humour in Prose

IN HIS FOREWORD to *Tatvamasi* written by Sukumar Azhikode, Ayyappa Paniker wrote:

> Where does that sound echo from? Where does that uninterrupted flow of words spring from? When we cock our ears to find the source of that verbal river—that begins with one round of applause from the listeners and dissolves into the next—we find a gaunt figure firmly holding the stem of the microphone with his left hand as if to prevent himself from falling, due to fatigue or enthusiasm. We realise that the man who depends on the microphone is Prof. Sukumar Azhikode.

Those who have seen Sukumar Azhikode and heard his rousing speeches cannot imagine a more delightful description than this. In order to experience the joy of sublime humour more fully, one has to read the entire Foreword. Let us go into a more pungent instance of Ayyappa Paniker's humour.

Introducing Karl Marx's *Das Kapital* in *Vishwa Sahithyangaliloode: 2* (Through World Literature: 2), published by DC Books, Ayyappa Paniker wrote:

> Even those economists, who state that whatever Marx said about surplus value and labour-based principle of value was wrong, will not be able to deny the global fame, relevance and popularity of Marx and *Das Kapital*. *Das Kapital* is a work that should be read even by Marxists (146).

Ayyappa Paniker developed the art of conveying the truth—in this case, that most people become Communists without reading and understanding *Das Kapital* and that many among Communists have not read *Das Kapital*—by couching it in spiky humour that would not hurt anyone. Just as there are Christians who have not read the Bible or Muslims who have not understood the Quran, there are many Communists who have not studied *Das Kapital*. Although Ayyappa Paniker uses very mild language to ridicule those who strut around as authoritative advocates of a philosophy without having read its foundational texts, his words convey his desire to see the mistake rectified.

Once, a student named Vinaya Kumar, who had earned his Master's degree in English with high marks, was advised by well-meaning teachers and friends to pursue research under a famous academic as that would further his job prospects. Maybe because of mounting pressure from them, he approached Ayyappa Paniker and expressed his interest in doing research. The interview began. Coming to the subject, Ayyappa Paniker asked, "Why do you want to go in for research?"

"For the experience of it."

"What do you mean? People do things to achieve an end. What is the end result that you are striving for?"

"No end result. I am doing it for its own sake ... I want to experience what research feels like. I don't particularly want a PhD."

Vinaya Kumar's voice was heavy with extreme self-confidence that his creditable marks had given him.

Clearing his throat, Ayyappa Paniker retorted, "Getting pregnant is enough. You don't want to deliver, eh? Splendid, very splendid!"

Vinaya Kumar realised that when his self-confidence had gone overboard, Ayyappa Paniker had used his natural wit to squash it. But he understood the corrective intent of Ayyappa Paniker's words only after he became a teacher himself. Vinaya Kumar describes this experience in his own style in *Ayyappa Paniker Forever* (60–61).

Ayyappa Paniker believed in the philosophy that criticism, if covered in humour, will not injure anyone. He wrote about Forewords in the beginning of his book titled *Krithiyum Porulum* ("Work and Essence"): "Considering that 'Forewords' are invariably intended more to show generosity to the works concerned than to introduce them to the readers, they are better described as 'Favours'[1]." Within the space of a single sentence, Ayyappa Paniker brought together both those who wait endlessly for Forewords and others who offer casual or empty promises to write them.

> There are many virgin-brides too, who, even after the books are printed, wait for forewords.... There are those who abscond with the manuscript, after promising to write a wonderful foreword. Apprehending such culprits is a tad difficult.

Jose Panachippuram, editor of *Malayala Manorama* and *Bhashaposhini*, and more significantly Ayyappa Paniker's student, feels that if one were to expand the initial in Ayyappa Paniker's name, "K" would read as *Kusrithi*[2] (rather than "Kesava Paniker")—an appropriate expansion, considering that mischief is a harmless joke that can yet hit the target.

In 1972, in the eleventh issue of *Kerala Kavitha*, Ayyappa Paniker wrote an article titled "*Bhoomiyude Oosharatwam*" (Barrenness of the Earth) in which he gave an amusing description of how poetry gets evaluated:

> This is a work that has blessed readers with troubles—troubles like ignorance in those who have not read it

---

1 Ayyappa Paniker plays on the words *Avathaarika* (meaning "Foreword" in Malayalam) and *Audaarika* (from *Audaaryam*, meaning "generosity/favour" in Malayalam).

2 "Mischievous" in Malayalam.

or anger in those who have read but not understood it. Many point to the narrative technique of *The Waste Land* as the flag staff of Modernism in world literature. Both its supporters and detractors (and other pen-pushers)[3] agree on this matter most of the time (As quoted in *Tharishubhumi*, Calicut: Mathrubhumi Books, 2023: 37).

In earlier times, when people wrote letters, they inserted the paper in an envelope and pasted the cover with the help of cooked rice. Once, Lakshmikutty Amma wrote a letter to her brother Ayyappa Paniker who was then far away, and stuck it in haste before posting. The reply came soon afterwards, assuring her, "I got your letter and the cooked rice." Humour came to him in a very natural and unforced manner, whether he wrote letters or composed creative pieces.

It accompanied his behaviour and gestures as well. Once, Vishnu Narayanan Namboothiri and Ayyappa Paniker participated in a poets' meet in a hall that was filled to overflowing. Vishnu Narayanan Namboothiri began to recite his poem. On the dais were Ayyappa Paniker and other poets, awaiting their turn. Tea was served in paper cups to all the poets seated on the stage. Vishnu Narayanan Namboothiri placed his cup on the lectern and totally immersed in his presentation, he attracted everyone's attention exclusively to himself.

---

3 Here too, the Malayali reader is struck by Ayyappa Paniker's play with words. He writes *anukoolikalum, prathikoolikalum* (*mattu koolikalum*). Translated into English, the force of the pun is lost!

In the course of his recitation, when he lifted his hand, it hit the cup and sent the tea out of the cup in a wide arc. When the liquid landed on Ayyappa Paniker's shirt, everyone on the dais as well as the audience went totally silent. The minutes that followed stretched like aeons. No one had a clue about what to do. Vishnu Narayanan Namboothiri's eyes, which always sparkled with spiritual poise, expressed agitation and self-reproach. The audience too became anxious. Vishnu Narayanan Namboothiri's guilt-ridden cries "Ayyo! Ayyo!" and piteous face melted everyone's heart.

"Don't worry, Vishnu. What's lost is lost. We'll order another cup of tea," Ayyappa Paniker's words of consolation caused the audience to break into laughter. He had bailed out not only Vishnu Narayanan Namboothiri but the entire crowd of aesthetes from a terribly embarrassing situation.

17
As a Vibrant Presence

WHEN WE RESEARCH Ayyappa Paniker in order to find out who he really was, seeking the opinions of those who worked with him is bound to make the mission more vibrant and honest. Let us go through the words spoken by his contemporaries and also a few writers who belonged to the next generation in order to find out how they viewed him.

Among those who are alive today (it may not be wrong to say, among those who are alive and dead), the person who was closest to him was the great Malayalam critic, M.K. Sanoo. He is prominent among the most popular litterateurs in Kerala and perhaps the person to have been invited as the chief guest in the largest number of cultural meetings. It was when he contested from the Ernakulam assembly constituency against a constantly winning party, yet won with a huge majority, that we realised his special ability to command respect not only from literature lovers but from all who came in contact with him. (In this context, I recall that Ayyappa Paniker, M.K. Sanoo and D.C. Kizhekkemuri, the writer, activist and book publisher, came together to attend my wedding to Jessy at Paingottoor village near Moovattupuzha in Ernakulam district in 1986.)

Although many people have written about Ayyappa Paniker, M.K. Sanoo must be the one who has written the most (the other may be Satchidanandan). M.K. Sanoo has authored two books, *Ayyappa Paniker: Nishedhathinte Charu Roopam* (Ayyappa Paniker: The Elegant Image of Defiance) and *Ayyappa Panikerum Ayyappa Panikerum* (Ayyappa Paniker and Ayyappa Paniker). The first book is a study of Ayyappa Paniker's life and poetry, viewing him as the creator of a new age in Malayalam poetry. The second is a peek into the multifaceted nature, power of influence and respectable traits of Ayyappa Paniker's personality.

Once, M.K. Sanoo expressed a wish to write a comprehensive biography of Ayyappa Paniker. In his view, there had been no one who was so inspirational as Ayyappa Paniker, and that was the reason why, despite Paniker being younger than him, M.K. Sanoo nursed that desire. John Paul, the screenplay writer, testified that M.K. Sanoo had written about the bond of mutual affection between himself and Ayyappa Paniker, and about Ayyappa Paniker as he knew him. The readers too admired the book as a celebration of respect between two great humans. He had known Ayyappa Paniker since 1950, and was a friend who supported him and cooperated with him in all cultural initiatives. It is this bond of friendship that he describes in *Ayyappa Panikerum Ayyappa Panikerum* (Ayyappa Paniker and Ayyappa Paniker).

> As a friend too, Ayyappa Paniker maintained utmost affection and sincerity. He used to establish friendship only with like-minded individuals. And there was purity in those bonds. The way in which he maintained friendship—without a trace of selfishness—and gave whatever support he could, was exemplary. Several instances of such exemplary friendships remain in my memory as fragrances. Even there, he kept his virtues as a secret pride, and that was his strength (46).

The people who most profited from his guidance were poets. He recognised that plants and flowers of various hues and smells were what imparted beauty and fragrance to the garden and the season of poetry he nurtured. He never persuaded anyone into pursuing any specific style. (He himself did not have such a style!) He opened the avenues of world poetry to those who accompanied or followed him, encouraged young poets to pave their own paths, and gave them a leg-up to climb the ladder towards excellence. Besides publishing the works of young poets in *Kerala Kavitha*, he gave all the support and cooperation required to bring out anthologies of their works. Ayyappa Paniker will be remembered forever for arousing the talents of and empowering all the poets of his time. He was a model not only in ensuring his own growth as a poet but also in living successfully as a good, socially committed individual. Let us go through what a few of his contemporaries said about him.

Vishnu Narayanan Namboothiri (1939–2021) was a writer who followed the N.V. Krishna Warrier school of poetry. As a poet, Ayyappa Paniker was not enamoured of it but he did everything possible to encourage the poetic spirit of Namboothiri. As the latter himself admitted, "Whenever he read a few poems [of mine] and enjoyed them, he would come all the way to my *illam* at Thiruvalla to talk to me. He had committed poems like '*Dileepan*' to memory (*Gurupuja*, 2022: 19).

Kadammanitta Ramakrishnan (1935–2008) was a poet like none other, whose recitals aroused the Malayalis to a frenzy of delight. Most Malayalis are very familiar with his poems like "*Shanta*", "*Kurathi*", "*Kattaalan*" and "*Kozhi*". He was five years younger than Ayyappa Paniker. When Ayyappa Paniker, lauded by M. Govindan in the mid-1960s as the most significant poet of Malayalam, wrote appreciatively about Kadammanitta in a special issue, it proved to be a shot in the arm for the latter and he openly admitted it. It was due to Ayyappa Paniker's encouragement that Kadammanitta translated Samuel Beckett's world-famous play *Waiting for Godot* into Malayalam, and Adoor Gopalakrishnan directed it on stage. I recall Ayyappa Paniker saying that the Malayalam translation of *Waiting for Godot* should be one of the first works to be brought out by Sankramanam Books, and how we did it. Kadammanitta observed that it was Ayyappa Paniker who inspired and helped him translate Octavio Paz's poem "Sunstone" 20 years before it won the Nobel Prize, and also the works of the Senegalese poet and former president of Senegal, Leopold Sedar Senghor, Spanish poet Federico Garcia Lorca, Peruvian poet and writer Cesar Vallejo and others.

When conservative writers and ideologues accused Ayyappa Paniker of being the evangelist of anarchy and misleading others, Kadammanitta retorted furiously. That was an index of his respect for Ayyappa Paniker:

> Having cooperated with him [Ayyappa Paniker] and participated actively in the fields of literature and culture, I can say categorically that, at least in my case, he has not misled me. He has only helped me move forward along the right path, with a clearer vision, more scientifically, and with a more heightened awareness of humanism. Humanism and freedom were the values he held aloft. He has not written even a single word that was not triggered by his social sense (*Kerala Kavitha*, 2007: 237).

Ayyappa Paniker not only had a sincere desire to see his loved ones and friends progress in life but he also worked enthusiastically towards making it possible. This was not an isolated characteristic but a quality that is testified to by many. Kadammanitta said:

> Interaction with him benefitted me in various ways. It was his nature to be anxious about his friends. He was interested in their family matters as well. My parents, wife and children loved him. Ayyappa Paniker was my elder brother (*Kerala Kavitha*, 2007: 240).

Satchidanandan was an English teacher at Christ's College, Irinjalakuda, and, as a poet, he galvanised the youth of Kerala. The collapse of a movement he had significantly helped build across Kerala deeply distressed him and led him to distance himself (to the point of severance) from Janakeeya Samskarika Vedi.[1] It was a herculean task for him to convince the young generation, who had followed in the footsteps of intellectuals like Satchidanandan and built their lives accordingly, of the reasoning behind his change of stance.

During this period of intense personal and public trauma in Satchidanandan's life, Ayyappa Paniker stepped in to ease his way into taking up the post of editor of *Indian Literature*, a publication of the Central Sahitya Akademi. What followed is known to all: step by step, Satchidanandan rose to the top position of the Sahitya Akademi and represented India at literary conferences abroad. It is true that he had the merit and the eligibility to grace those posts. Before Satchidanandan left for Delhi to take up the Central Sahitya Akademi assignment, Ayyappa Paniker put him in touch with Bharat Bhavan at Bhopal. It was perhaps from there that Satchidanandan's flourishing connections with other Indian and international poets fructified, which Satchidanandan acknowledges as a significant turning point in his life.

K. Ayyappa Paniker was a poet, translator, critic, editor, scholar and teacher. Satchidanandan also became a poet, translator, critic, editor, polyglot and teacher, but he was entirely different from Ayyappa Paniker in the style he adopted and the stances he took. Satchidanandan was not a student who sat in Ayyappa Paniker's class—rather, he grew under the guidance and encouragement of Ayyappa Paniker

---

1 A cultural forum run by the then Naxalites of Kerala.

as he himself has said in unequivocal terms in his speeches and articles. Ayyappa Paniker was aware that those who accompanied and followed him in his poetic path were not necessarily like him, and was insistent that they should not be so. After all, a person who was "[a]ll his life ... patiently learning how not to live at all"² would hardly want his pupils to toe his line. It was this magnanimity, sublimity, perspective and approach that made him a great guide. Perhaps that was the reason he had such a vast circle of disciples.

Satchidanandan has often said that from very early in his life, although he was interested in translating poetry, it was Ayyappa Paniker who made him understand that the exercise of translation—be it from English to Malayalam or vice versa—was as important as writing poetry. The truth is that Ayyappa Paniker detected a very good translator in Satchidanandan, and encouraged him to the fullest extent. Satchidanandan has written:

> Paniker would never directly mentor anyone. But he had an intuitive way of understanding the way their individual genius worked and of gently prodding them to discover their own style (*Indian Quarterly*, 2020 October).

Deshamangalam Ramakrishnan who joined University College, Thiruvananthapuram as a teacher in 1984, got acquainted with Ayyappa Paniker and in the course of

---

2 A line from his famous poem "*Maranakkurippu*" ("Epitaph", *Selected Poems of Ayyappa Paniker*, Modern Book Centre, 1985: 56).

time, their friendship grew. Ayyappa Paniker soon started entrusting Deshamangalam Ramakrishnan with the task of translating works from other languages for publication in *Kerala Kavitha*. Shortly thereafter, Ayyappa Paniker made him shoulder the responsibility of being the associate editor of *Kerala Kavitha*. When the informal poetic forum of *Sankramanam* was formed in 1995, Ramakrishnan was made its chief organiser. In this manner, Ayyappa Paniker prodded and nourished the poet, the translator, the literary critic and the editor in Ramakrishnan. This was what he had to say about his life in Thiruvananthapuram and his interactions with Ayyappa Paniker:

> That was the time when I had left the troubles of my native village and come to the travails of city life. A hassle-free closeness—that was what I learnt from Paniker sir's behaviour. I got a reprieve from a lonely existence as well as a refuge in life and in poetry. Such an attitude was not reserved for me alone. He was like this to others as well. What sir tried to do was nurture such discoveries, and never to snuff them. That was an endless fount of energy. With his no-strings-attached attitude, he set me ablaze, and inspired me to continue glowing. This can be described as a *guru-shishya* bond, a friendship or a family relationship (*Mathrubhumi* newspaper, 2006, August 24: 12).

It was only natural for a person of such a sattvic temperament as Deshamangalam Ramakrishnan to accept Ayyappa Paniker as his *guru*.

Observe what K.G.S. (K.G. Sankara Pillai, the academic, poet, editor and translator) had to say about Ayyappa Paniker in the course of a speech delivered online in 2021:

> Among the minds that influenced me profoundly and energised me, the most prominent one is perhaps Ayyappa Paniker sir. In 1981, at a time when I least desired it and in the most unexpected manner, he announced that my early poems would be compiled and published as a *Kerala Kavitha* publication. That was a huge gesture of encouragement, acknowledgement and acceptance. Paniker sir granted me an experience of great strength, as though he had held me by my hand and raised me to the vast world of poetry.

When K.G.S. states that he was introduced to many writers, especially those from other languages, there are several who share similar experiences. Such forging of links was a noteworthy feature of Ayyappa Paniker's humanistic creative work.

> I cannot forget how he encouraged me, during my years of poetic drought, by constantly writing letters (some of which were penned at Madras, Hyderabad, Delhi, Kolkata or California on notepads from hotels in which he stayed, sometimes with his illustrations on the margins) or gifting me books of poetry on return after travel (*Bhashaposhini*, 2006: 21).

He, like Kadammanitta, underscores the fact that Ayyappa Paniker took interest in his family matters as well: "When my mother was afflicted with Alzheimer's disease, he would enquire after her from time to time. He used to say that all we have is memory, and everything hangs from the thread of that life-breath" (*Bhashaposhini*, 2006, October: 20).

Ayyappa Paniker's most vibrant friendships were with the poets of the newest generation. And that was astonishing indeed. He would interact with the student-poets at schools and colleges as though they were his equals. He freely cracked jokes in their company and accompanied them to poetry-reading sessions. K.G.S. describes it like this:

> Paniker's inner preparedness was such that he was always ahead of his times, never behind the newest generation of writers either in the use of an image, a tune or an idea. Rare indeed are those who can gel with even the youngest poets with such ease (*Bhashaposhini*, 2006, October: 20).

Shanthan, one of the most notable poets in Malayalam today has this to say, while considering the vastness of contemporary Malayalam poetry:

> There was enough space for all kinds of poems in the expansive poetic skies of Ayyappa Paniker. It should not be forgotten that no one else in the history of Malayalam poetry had such a wide perspective. Bringing poetry from the idealistic world to the real one was a task that he was engaged in throughout his life. It should not be forgotten that it was Ayyappa Paniker who gave support to the eclecticism of contemporary Malayalam poetry that catered to the varied aesthetic tastes of the fisherman, the mason, the

vegetable vendor, the Adivasi, the sea-faring folk and the autorickshaw driver (*Madhyamam* weekly, 2020, September: 56).

The poet and literary analyst T.P. Rajeevan is of the opinion that Ayyappa Paniker would definitely have influenced individuals and institutions connected to the field of culture, especially poetry:

> In many ways, Ayyappa Paniker was not a mere individual. He was a presence. Paniker did on his own what academies, literary and cultural institutions and universities ought to do. He gave the rest the task of managing such institutions (*Bhashaposhini*, 2006, October: 29).

Ayyappa Paniker became an influential powerhouse not merely by climbing the steps of excellence as a poet and literary person but, more importantly, by imparting energy and confidence to other poets and writers so that they could climb the steps too.

C.S. Jayachandran, poet and journalist, encapsulates Ayyappa Paniker's personality in a single sentence: "There is only once escape route open to any contemporary Malayalam poet from the influence of Ayyappa Paniker. That is not to read him" (*Ayyappa Paniker: Jeevitharekha* [Ayyappa Paniker: Life Sketch], DC Books, 2007: 72).

18
Outlook on Life

ONE EVENING IN 1988, Ayyappa Paniker and his wife paid us a visit. We had not been informed earlier, so the visit took us by surprise. When they sat down, Ayyappa Paniker's wife said, "We went to Karikkakam temple, and on our way back thought of stepping in." After they left, I was haunted by a query: Was Ayyappa Paniker a believer in God? I had never heard him mention God in his conversations or speeches. I knew this was not a topic that should bother me, but it did because I had not thought of him a religious person.

In due course, my interest in the subject petered out because whether he was a believer or not did not really matter to me and my thoughts on that aspect of his life came to a halt. Later, when I began my enquiries about who Ayyappa Paniker really was, I plied the members of his family as well as his friends with several questions. Ayyappa Paniker's daughter and others said that he used to go to temples occasionally.

> O my God,
> who may or may not be,
> in your existential angst,
> will you have time
> to face me?
>
> O Master,
> If you exist not,
> won't you please
> redirect this prayer
> to the dead letter office? ("*Praarthana*" ["Prayer"])

When I decided to go through his poems, I did not get any specific answer. His poems gave the impression that he was a non-believer:

> Aha!
> God and One
> God and Two
> God and Three
> God and Four
> When he came to God and Five
> Shouted I: You stop
> Your lousy singsong!
> Look around yourself:
> Man is still benumbed,

> Man's veil is on sale,
> Man sneaks into hiding.
> If you have tears still.
> Shed them now. ("*Deivathonnu*", ["God and One," *Days and Nights*, NERC, 2001: 75).

He loved the people he saw rather than the God he did not. Whether he believed in God or not, he believed in humans. I had not heard anyone say that he set apart time or money for God. But I have heard from many beneficiaries that he spent not only a lot of time and money on them but also intervened for their welfare. Was his religion humanism?

T.S. Eliot's *The Waste Land* in all likelihood inspired Ayyappa Paniker, but while Eliot portrayed a world of hopelessness, Ayyappa Paniker saw a hopeful future. *The Waste Land* and *Kurukshetram* present two perspectives on life. The pessimistic approach that we see informing Eliot's poetry is absent in *Kurukshetram* and other poems by Ayyappa Paniker. In fact, he once voiced the opinion that Eliot's inability to see a brave and energetic humankind was rather unhealthy. "*Polla Manushyaraanu Chuttum*" ("Around Us are Hollow Men") in *Ayyappa Panikerude Lekhanangal: 1950–80* (Ayyappa Paniker's Prose Writings: 1950–80) [DC Books, 1985: 35] was not a philosophy that Ayyappa Paniker espoused. Not only in works like "*Kurukshetram*", "Hey, Gagarin!", "*Agnipuja*" ("Fire Worship") and "*Martyapuja*" ("Hymn to Man") but also in his last collection "*Pathumanippookkal*" ("Poetry at Midnight"), he presented his belief in human beings and humanism.

> ...who, pray, hies to the sacred Bodhi tree
> for the torch that will cast the needed light?
> If the soul is illumined
> who has to speak
> of the Mount of Calvary?
> If indeed for a rare moment
> we could all just human be ... (*"Kurukshetram"*, Selected Poems of Ayyappa Paniker, Modern Book Centre, 1985: 27–28).

Rather than go to temples and churches, carry out *puja*s or prayer ceremonies, follow traditions and perform rituals, it is better to be moral and kind people. We have to internalise humanism, and look at our fellow creatures through that prism.

Born into a caste-bound social environment, Ayyappa Paniker lacked the affection of his Namboodiri father and was devastated by his mother's death during his teenage years. But when problems and challenges arose in life, Ayyappa Paniker refused to be a victim. He confronted them all, and moved on in life without withdrawing or surrendering in fear. Armed with affection, courage and goodness, he ploughed his own furrow. His was a life driven constantly by enthusiasm. He was determined not to fall into traps set to destroy him, and he overcame the odds. As Ayyappa Paniker wrote in *"Ente Bhithimel"* ("Upon My Walls"):

> Look at the picture my hands have drawn on my walls:
> Why do you stare? Look carefully, you fool! (Selected Poems of Ayyappa Paniker, Modern Book Centre, 1985: 9).

On reading this poem, written in 1952, along with "*Chakram*" ("The Wheel") composed 50 years later during the last phase of his life, one fact emerges clearly. Born as we are without our consent, the screenplay of our life is written by someone unknown, according to which we live and die. But we can make powerful interventions, and bring about corrections and modifications in the screenplay. That was what Ayyappa Paniker did. Instead of falling in line with the scripted screenplay, he kept on making corrections. And, to a very large extent, he succeeded in his mission.

> Born somewhere,
> Growing up somewhere,
> You and I are destined
> To fall down somewhere.
> In between
> A slight drizzle,
> The touch of a peacock feather,
> Shadow of a rainbow,
> A slice of moonlight,
> A play of the eyes.
> Over. The wheel stops rotating.
> So, friend,
> Consider this as our auspicious moment.
> Don't waste it.
> Don't share it with anyone. ("The Wheel," trans. P. Ravindran Nayar, *Poetry at Midnight*, Folio, 2010: 54).

19
Wake-up Calls in the Field of Painting

IN 1993, WHEN Ayyappa Paniker attended our housewarming ceremony, he gifted us with a painting by the prominent artist—B.D. Dathan. Roughly four feet long and three feet wide, it has been framed and mounted in such a way that we and every visitor and resident notices it all the time. The painting telescopes the themes of *The Waste Land* and *Kurukshetram*. The desert of *The Waste Land* and the leafless but life-promising tree of *Kurukshetram* are captured in it. The painting is so evocative that it contains possibilities of meanings that are likely to be different from the one I see. Neither Dathan who painted it nor the poet who gifted it, the people who have already seen it and those who are yet to view it may agree with my observation about the painting. But hasn't Ayyappa Paniker himself said that once the process of creation is over and the work reaches the aesthete, the creator's hold on its meaning(s) ceases and the public takes over?

In *Ayyappa Paniker: Jeevitharekha* (Ayyappa Paniker: Life Sketch), B.D. Dathan has admitted that Ayyappa Paniker was a person who wielded tremendous influence not only on his artistic works but on his life as well. More significantly, Ayyappa Paniker encouraged him in a substantial way too. Once, in the course of a conversation, Dathan even said that if he were to be born again, he wished to be more closely associated with Ayyappa Paniker and work along with him.

> My long association with Ayyappa Paniker is one of the fortunes I have enjoyed in my artistic life. He was a *guru* for all time, not a mere teacher or a poet. He was a movement that encompassed many talents, and led the way forward constantly. It is not possible to see another poet or litterateur in our time who encouraged up-and-coming poets and litterateurs as much as Ayyappa Paniker did. I have not heard him utter a single discouraging word to anyone, anytime. The words that came out of Ayyappa Paniker's lips, that were always couched in humour, were profoundly meaningful (*B.D. Dathante Vaakkum Varayum*, Kerala Bhasha Institute, 2021: 167).

Lizzie Jacob, who was the chief secretary of Kerala, described Ayyappa Paniker as a person who influenced her even without her being aware of it. A member of the Advisory Board of Kochi Biennale, she is also an artist of independent repute.

I have personally seen and realised how he has lent support and shade to blossoming buds. The ease with which he is able to interact with all in a spirit of democracy, across differences in status, age and nationality, has always amazed me. He was a person who walked the highway but he took the trouble of holding many by the hand from the by-lanes, and leading them to the main road. It is definitely a task that most people dare not do (*Kerala Kavitha*, 2007: 219–20).

Ayyappa Paniker granted unconditional support to the Suryakanti Trust in Thiruvananthapuram, headed by Lizzie Jacob, for the promotion of fine arts, particularly painting and sculpture, and the organising of appreciation camps. Ms Jacob admitted that Ayyappa Paniker worked as the unofficial president of the Suryakanti Trust, and attended all its meetings, leaving a personal stamp on all its activities.

It was Ayyappa Paniker himself who drew illustrations for his cartoon poems and maharaja tales, compiled and published in 1982. Seven years later, when *Gotrayanam* ("Southbound") was published, he drew the picture for its cover page. Besides, the book carried his illustrations in all its 23 pages. He was a complete artist who had interest in and talent for literature, music and traditional art forms as well as painting.

The famous sculptors and painters of Kerala—M.V. Devan and Kanayi Kunhiraman—were Ayyappa Paniker's close friends and received immense encouragement and support from him in their creative lives. It was M.V.

Devan who wrote a detailed critical piece as the Foreword for Ayyappa Paniker's anthology of poems published by Navadhara in 1974.

The Malayali artist Vishwanathan, who resides permanently in Paris, is a great admirer of Ayyappa Paniker. He took great pride in arranging a French translation of "*Pookkathirikkan Enikkaavathille*" ("I Can't Help Blossoming") and submitting it for a French award. The eponymous poem written in the poet's hand is a permanent exhibit at the famous Musee d'Art Contemporain du Val-de-Marne (Contemporary Art Museum of Val-de-Marne) in France, among other selected works of world poetry.

As in the field of literature, in painting too, Ayyappa Paniker showed his allegiance to iconoclasts. Advocates of contemporary painting like Riyas Komu and Bose Krishnamachari not only speak reverentially about Ayyappa Paniker but have also included profile pictures of him in their collections.

20
World Malayali

THE RENOWNED PRODUCER of Malayalam films, Kulathur Bhaskaran Nair, constructed a building with a hall named "Chitrapuram" at Maruthamkuzhi in Thiruvananthapuram in order to host cultural programmes. We used to conduct discussions on various topics in that hall. It was there that the first edition of Ayyappa Paniker's historic *Gotrayanam* ("Southbound") was released. Copies of the deluxe edition of the work, autographed by the author, were available for everyone who attended the function that day in 1989. It contained 23 illustrations by Ayyappa Paniker. The official release took place with the veteran film actor Madhu reciting the first of the 12 cantos of the poem. The USP of the hardbound book (25 x 19 cm) was the illustration on its cover page, drawn by the poet himself.

Bhaskaran Nair took the initiative to conduct meetings in this hall in order to provide a common platform for

Malayalis scattered all over the world so that they could contribute something to the land of their birth. Many, including Ayyappa Paniker and Priyan C. Oommen, who was a cultural activist, found the idea very attractive. But there were doubts too as to whether such discussions among a few people at Maruthamkuzhi would bear any fruit.

While such misgivings were being raised, two Malayalis from the US came to India with a similar idea. Their plan was to have a World Malayali Convention at New Jersey. The two men were John Abraham, the first Malayali mayor in the US, and Andrew Pappachan, public activist and chief engineer of the water supply department of New Jersey. The person they met first in order to moot the subject was M.A. Baby, then a Rajya Sabha member living in Delhi. On his advice, they spoke to B.C. Jojo, the Thiruvananthapuram bureau chief of *Kerala Kaumudi*. The latter suggested that instead of a convention, if they could conceive of a system like a council for the welfare of world Malayalis, cooperation would definitely be forthcoming. The idea was acceptable and soon a convention for the formation of a World Malayali Council was decided upon. In accordance with these plans, we started discussions with B.C. Jojo, Priyan C. Oommen, John Mundakkayam of the *Malayala Manorama*, D. Babu Paul who was the additional chief secretary and others.

Decisions were taken to conduct a World Malayali Convention at New Jersey on 1, 2 and 3 July 1995, and send a delegation of 40 individuals from Kerala to the US. We also decided that the individuals forming the team should be prominent people. Accordingly, we selected film actors like Madhu and Innocent, senior journalists like Thomas Jacob (*Malayala Manorama*), Rajagopal (*Mathrubhumi*) and Abraham (*Deepika*), cultural leaders like Ayyappa Paniker and others.

The plan was to begin the journey from Thiruvananthapuram, fly to Bombay, and then proceed to New York after a few hours. The departure from Thiruvananthapuram went as scheduled. Air Travel Enterprises, a prominent travel agent in Kerala, had assured us that the ticket reservation would be confirmed in Bombay. Although there was some risk involved, we took the leap of faith. However, even after we reached Bombay, there was no confirmation. As the organisers, we started to feel stressed due to the presence of several VIPs in the group. Finally, we decided to inform them of the situation.

Later, Jojo described the situation in *Kala Kaumudi* like this:

> On hearing that the reservation to New York was not confirmed, everyone became uneasy as time passed—except for one person. The image of the smiling Paniker sir, seated in the departure lounge and consoling Priyadas and others who were walking around in an agitated manner, will never fade from my mind (*Kala Kaumudi*, 206, September: 19).

Ayyappa Paniker, who understood the source of the problem—the organisers' lack of experience and the large size of the group—stood by us and cooperated with us. Instead of standing apart like a VIP, he became one of us.

The relief he provided us and the other guests, along with the lightness he brought into the situation in order to counter our stress, was significant. Eventually, as promised by the travel agent, everything came through at the last moment, and we could continue our journey.

However, even after the meeting began, there were several unexpected glitches, but at each and every such instance, Ayyappa Paniker's innate humour and contextual jokes helped us handle the problems in a casual manner. He remarked that it was "World Malayali Confusion" and, during a moment of crisis, even quipped that it was a "World Malayali Convulsion" taking place in America! When he returned, he wrote a poem titled "*Loka Malayali*" ("World Malayali").

Much before all this came through, when the idea of "World Malayali" was only incubating, someone asked Ayyappa Paniker to write a prayer song, just before a meeting on the subject was about to begin. He immediately penned one, and handed it over to M.K. Gopalakrishnan, the actor. It was titled "*Aandupirappoli*" ("New Year Greetings"). There are many organisations that use it as their theme song!

As its first line "May everyone, everyone be blessed" seemed to transfer all its emotional fulness from the poet to Gopalakrishnan, when the latter sang it, each member of the audience could feel the tide of blessings wash over them. Robert Frost once remarked that words in deeply thought out poems will have one or more than one meaning. The words in most of Ayyappa Paniker's poems have more than one meaning and sometimes even convey the opposite of what they seem to say! But this poem, that is free of multiple meanings, symbols, figures of speech or other ornaments, conveys his philosophy in the simplest possible manner:

> "New Year Greetings"
>
> May everyone, everyone be blessed.
> May the haves and the have-nots prosper.
> May the male and the female be blessed.
> May the sea and the earth prosper.
> May the land and its residents be blessed.
> May the forest and its inmates prosper.
> May the small and the big be blessed.
> May those living abroad also prosper.
> May we and you be blessed.
> May we all prosper.

He knew that not only the marginalised but everyone going through crises would require attention, consideration, caress and support. That is what the poem "New Year Greetings" communicates to us. Linguistic scholarship and literary theories sat light on his shoulders. Precisely for that reason, he could write very simple poems.

This poem has been the prayer song for several years at the stress-free school named "Sandepani," managed by K.G. Vijayalakshmi in Thiruvananthapuram. It is the theme song of "Altius," a youth collective that aims to raise the social commitment of the students of Kerala to international levels.

Basic Malayalam

There arose a demand in many countries for a system that would help new generations of Malayalis learn their mother tongue. In response to this, a workshop involving E.M.S.,[1] O.N.V., Babu Paul, Ayyappa Paniker and others was organised in the meeting hall at Mascot Hotel, Thiruvananthapuram. Besides Malayalam language scholars, many teachers and writers participated in it. Subsequently, under the leadership of Ayyappa Paniker, a team comprising college teachers like M.S. Balakrishnan Nair and Sreedevi K. Nair, K.M. Lenin of the Malayalam Lexicon Department and K.X. Raju of the *Sankramanam* editorial team was created. They met on Sunday afternoons and decided on the contents of the book.

Through this project, Ayyappa Paniker gave no explicit lessons on selfless leadership, commitment and total dedication. Rather, he led by example. For more than six months, he came every Sunday for the meeting, and gave the members of this team all the required energy and knowledge, peppering it with memorable jokes, without however loosening his hold on the seriousness of the project. To this day, I savour the experience of picking him up from home and taking him back during those months.

While this was certainly an enterprise dedicated to the cause of promoting Malayalam, and designed to benefit the young generations of world Malayalis, Ayyappa Paniker's

---

1 E.M. Sankaran Namboodiripad, the first communist chief minister of the state of Kerala.

untiring efforts and practical leadership in taking it forward inspired us to strive, without letting our spirits flag, and also lent us invaluable strength. He kept on reminding us that the act of preserving our language, literature and culture was equivalent to helping expatriate Malayalis, scattered all over the globe, maintain their very identity.

The book was named *Basic Malayalam*. Each page carried three columns. In the right column was a letter of the Malayalam alphabet, a word, a sentence, or sometimes even a paragraph. Its exact English translation was given in the column on the left. In the middle was the corresponding English transliteration of the Malayalam segment. Nearly all the conversational bits included in the book were words, sentences and idioms of everyday use that could be used according to the context. Perhaps because of that factor, the government brought out a pocket edition of the book, and distributed copies of it among all the government tourist outlets for the benefit of visiting foreign tourists too.

21

A Gentle Presence

SANKRAMANA KAVITHA VEDI (Sankramana Poetry Forum) was a cultural platform initiated by Ayyappa Paniker in order to encourage novices and to impart energy to established voices in the field of poetry. He had not expressed any opinion about the name we had chosen for our little magazine during the time we ran it (1979–85) or even later, but when he selected it for an enterprise of this kind, we were extremely delighted.

The first meeting of Sankramana Kavitha Vedi took place at the Hindi Prachar Sabha Hall in Thiruvananthapuram in 1995. Such meetings were conducted every month, and provided a space for famous and unknown poets as well as beginners to present their works, listen to others and participate in discussions on them. The convenor of the programme was Deshamangalam Ramakrishnan, a poet, translator, critic and teacher at the Department of Malayalam, University of Kerala. He would send postcards to all members indicating the name of the guest poet of the forthcoming meeting, the title of the anthology from which its author would be presenting a poem or two, and other details. As he was a teacher at the department in the Karyavattam campus of the university, a few students were always there, ready to help him.

Ayyappa Paniker's noble intent and Deshamangalam Ramakrishnan's commitment were evident in these postcards. As everybody knew that both of them would reach the venue on time, the guest poets and the audience were careful to be present before the programme began. There were more than 50 members attending every meeting and sometimes, the number went up to a hundred too. We never missed the tea during the interval between poetry-reading sessions and discussions.

Every month, we listened to different poets as they recited pieces from their latest anthologies. The discussions revolving around those poems formed the centrepiece of our meetings, but the chief attraction of Sankramana Kavitha Vedi was undoubtedly the gentle presence of Ayyappa Paniker. At every meeting, we saw him encourage each participant with a look, a word or a gesture, and the poet concerned accepted it gratefully as a special acknowledgement meant exclusively for him/her. Ayyappa Paniker knew each one by their name, and took care to give each of them opportunities to present their talent, with little thought about their stature.

To those who were reluctant to participate in the discussions, Ayyappa Paniker would say, "Speak up, speak up lest you should lose sleep over the missed chance!" This short and humorous sentence was not merely meant to prod hesitant members, but served as a warning that later they should not feel uneasy about not having aired their opinion. Sometimes I wondered at the aggression shown by those who spoke on such occasions, but never saw Ayyappa Paniker throw a lasso around their necks. His policy was to permit every person to reveal his/her true self. (In those days, there were no forums where all the listeners received permission to speak out their thoughts. The situation is not very different today either.) But as there were no formalities at the Sankramana Kavitha Vedi, everybody enjoyed great freedom.

I do not know whether all the poets who attended our meetings returned completely satisfied. But everyone will agree that this style of Ayyappa Paniker's inspired all the poets of the new generation as well as the audience to become creative, to be remembered and to work enthusiastically. Even as poets recited their works, arguments became animated and discussions set the floor on fire, Ayyappa Paniker remained silent, like an ordinary member of the audience. But his presence was enough to keep the event within limits. Not only did he concede that all ideologies should be given their due space but he also honoured everyone's right to express their opinions. Even the poet Ayyappan, who was invariably drunk, recited his poems when he came as a guest, answered the questions shot at him, and behaved like a lamb, meek and mild.

Akkitham (Akkitham Achutan Namboothiri), Koothattukulam Mary John, Sugathakumari, Kavalam Narayana Panicker, Attoor Ravi Varma, Kilimanoor Remakanthan, Satchidanandan, K.G. Sankara Pillai, Deshamangalam Ramakrishnan, Balachandran Chullikkad, Ezhacheri Ramachandran, P. Narayana Kurup, O.V. Usha, Lalitha Lenin, Kilimanoor Madhu, Rati Saxena, the next generation of poets like Sebastian, Kureepuzha Sreekumar, Shanthan Haridasan, Vinod Vaishakhi, C.S. Jayachandran, Sajeev Kumar, Girish Puliyoor, T.P. Rajeevan, Jose Vaimeli, Manamboor Rajan Babu, K.R. Tony, P.Y. Balan, Asim Thannimood, R. Manoj, M.M. Sacheendran, Chayam Dharmarajan, Preetha Sasidharan, Indira Krishnan, Ambidas Karet, Uzhamalakkal Maitheen, Jayakrishnan Vaypur and countless other poets presented their works at Sankramana Kavitha Vedi. The comments made by critics like Kalarkode Vasudevan Nair, K.S. Rajasekharan, P. Soman, Dominic J. Kattoor, C.R. Prasad, M.N. Rajan, S. Shifa, T.K. Santhoshkumar, P. Gopakumar, C. Ashokan, Suresh R., P. Sasankan, M.K. Lenin, H.K. Santhosh and Vidhu Narayanan lent muscle and gravitas to the discussions, and made the sessions hugely meaningful.

By bringing poets and critics together on the same platform, Ayyappa Paniker introduced a new rhythm and dimension to the process of poetry appreciation. He also experimented with the possibility of providing creative feedback to cultural activists. Sankramana Kavitha Vedi hosted three generations of poets. It was a cultural movement led by Ayyappa Paniker and choreographed by Deshamangalam Ramakrishnan to strengthen the voices of young poets and literary observers. As mentioned earlier, the attempt to bring together young poets along with famous ones was started by Sankramana Kavitha Vedi in 1995.

In 1991, under Ayyappa Paniker's leadership, *Kerala Kavitha* reappeared as an annual magazine. That year's issue focused on postmodernism. At a time when established weeklies and magazines were reluctant to publish the works of young poets, Ayyappa Paniker brought out *Kerala Kavitha*, which contained the works of the latest poets, especially those who could not boast of high academic accomplishments, in order to give them a boost. M.M. Basheer, the publisher, has said that Ayyappa Paniker was an editor who published all the poems that were sent to him without editing them or even correcting the mistakes.

On the occasion of every new year, young poets from all over Kerala, under Ayyappa Paniker's leadership, assembled at a certain place, then asked the youngest contributor to recite his/her poem and release that year's issue of *Kerala Kavitha*. The magazine has been released in nearly all the districts of our state. Every young poet enjoyed the release function as an invaluable opportunity to spend an entire day in the company of a senior poet who enjoyed the status of a *guru* in their hearts. Most of the Malayalam poets who are famous today have taken this particular path. Nearly all the poets of the modernist and postmodernist phases of Malayalam poetry are always proud to acknowledge that they cut their teeth at *Kerala Kavitha*.

Just as Ayyappa Paniker never used Sankramana Kavitha Vedi to present his poems, he also did not allow

Kerala Kavitha to carry his poems while he was its editor. His intent was never to showcase himself. Instead, his aim was to ensure that everyone had their own opportunity to shine. The role of a guiding light was uniquely Ayyappa Paniker's to play in forums like Sankramana Kavitha Vedi or *Kerala Kavitha*. He focused on uncovering the potential in his fellow travellers and creating the right circumstances for them to flower. His goal was not to create followers or to have others imitate him. Ayyappa Paniker may not have imagined that he had the right or authority to dictate how others should shape their compositions.

22
Guild Soft

K.P.P. NAMBIAR AND Ayyappa Paniker were invited to inaugurate my software company named Guild Soft, by lighting the traditional lamp. My choice of K.P.P. Nambiar was praised because he was famous for being instrumental in laying the foundation for science and technology in Kerala by establishing KELTRON and Technopark. But I had to give a logical explanation to a few of the engineer colleagues in my company for inviting Ayyappa Paniker since they thought that he was invited because he was a well-wisher and teacher of the managing director.

I knew that he was not only fascinated by and had a special affinity with everything new, be it in matters of imagination or technology, but had an interest in studying and imbibing it too. He could step forward from the era of telephones to that of emails and the internet without any fear or hesitation whatsoever.

When S.E. James retired from service as a teacher of Malayalam from Malabar Christian College, Kozhikode, it was decided that a souvenir should be published to honour him. Dr K.V. Thomas, who represented the Souvenir Committee, asked Ayyappa Paniker, who was an alumnus of the college (he had studied there from 1946 to '48), to contribute an article. When Ayyappa Paniker emailed him the article, Dr Thomas replied that he could not read it as the script resembled the Greek alphabet! Ayyappa Paniker remarked that "Revathi" could solve the problem. While Dr Thomas was utterly flummoxed[1] Ayyappa Paniker told him that he had typed the matter using the Malayalam font named "Revathi". Therefore, downloading the same font in Dr Thomas's computer would solve the problem.

That was the time when Malayalam fonts had just become available. Thus, even before the birth of the new millennium, Ayyappa Paniker had begun to compose his poems on his computer. While new models of computers arrived in the market, he enquired about their configuration and other details as well as their advantages. I kept nagging him to purchase a new computer as prices were coming down year by year. Finally, he gagged me with a joke, "Be patient for some more time. If, as you say, the prices are coming down, that time is not far away when I can buy it without paying any money!"

In 1998, *Kerala Kaumudi* decided to bring out an online English edition of its paper. The internet edition editor B.C.

---

1 "Revathi" is a girl's name popular in Kerala.

Jojo was in charge of the project. In his words, "The first person I discussed the matter with was Paniker sir. The number of new ideas he shared with me was simply astounding!"

In 1994, in the initial phase of the internet, Ayyappa Paniker read the short story titled "Thingalaazhchakalile Aakaasham" ("The Sky on Mondays") written by Sethu (A. Sethumadhavan).[2] Sethu records in his autobiography that Ayyappa Paniker's comment on reading it was "Sethu has begun to see the future" and adds, "Wasn't Ayyappa Paniker himself a great savant who, by his meditative powers, could see the future?" (*Mathrubhumi* weekly, July 2022: 65).

I always knew that Ayyappa Paniker was a person who promoted everything new. That was why I always went to see him, hold discussions, and seek his blessings and prayers before I went to Europe, America and Japan to attend business meetings of my software company, Guild Soft. Before I set out on each trip, I spoke to him about the people I would be meeting. That was how I came into close contact with the painter Velu Viswanathan who stayed in Paris. The jobs I gave to a few people at Guild Soft on Ayyappa Paniker's recommendations, were my *guru dakshina*s or offerings to my teacher and mentor.

---

2   A. Sethumadhavan (b. 1942) is a very popular novelist and short story writer in Malayalam who has won numerous state awards for his novels. Some of his works are *Pandavapuram*, *Niyogam*, *Ezham Pakkam*, *Kaimudrakal* and *Marupiravi*, among others.

23
A Self-Respecting Individual

AFTER OUR WORK on the website centred on the topic of Ayyappa Paniker got completed, we showed the pages to him in order to get his consent before uploading them. He read it from beginning to end, and remarked, "Fine!" Then he asked us remove a word we had used to describe him. In the sentence "Ayyappa Paniker is a great Malayalam poet of the post-independence era," he took objection to the word "great" and demanded its deletion. I countered him with the argument, "That is for the readers to decide." But he stuck to his guns. "That is not for present-day readers like you to decide. That right belongs to the generation which will come 25 or 50 years after you." Although we tried our best to retain the word, he did not relent, and ensured it was deleted on the spot.

We live amidst many people who promote and market themselves. In this world, where nearly everyone scrambles to establish their own importance, Ayyappa Paniker demanded that we delete "great"! The computer programmer who was by my side while the conversation took place, was amazed at Ayyappa Paniker's humility. Many newspapers have written about Ayyappa Paniker going to the ration shop to purchase kerosene, dressed merely in a single-layered *mundu* and a slack shirt.

There was not a trace of self-praise in his speeches or conversations. Come to think of it, how could a man who was indifferent to his own sense of self, ever indulge in self-praise? Forget self-praise, first-person pronouns like "I", "me" and "my" were never part of his vocabulary. Whenever he used them in poetry, it was to denigrate rather than to praise himself.

"Just because I have stolen a few things, why should you call me a thief?"

"Protect me, this boring person!"

"I too tried to laugh/but no sound issued from my lips."

"I am a self-sacrificing person."

Poems like these, which contain instances of black humour, serve to prove this point.

Even when he described his mother's demise in "*Mrityudarshanam*" ("A Glimpse of Death"), he was especially careful to avoid words like "my" or "me":

> Death kept hovering in the neighbouring houses, among distant relatives and friends. At the age of

12 or 13, once again, saw death step into the house. A clear memory. Saw mother's mother and mother getting snuffed out, the oil dried up. Also saw invisible hands pull down the wick. "On the pomegranate the eight-petalled flower/blossomed abruptly, fell off its stalk into grief."[1] That was a horrendous death-dance. Unfathomable depths. With that came, freedom from fear. Whatever happened thereafter, what did it matter? Went to sleep every night bearing memories of having lived several lives (*Ayyappa Panikerude Lekhanangal: 1950–80* [Ayyappa Paniker's Prose Writings: 1950–80], DC Books, 1985: 303).

In *Vyaktichitrangal Yatradrishyangal* (Personal Profiles, Travel Sights), Ayyappa Paniker wrote thus:

The first-person pronoun appears in some articles. The third-person pronoun in one or two. Therefore, an anticipatory request – please do not take offence.

This apology, sought in advance, comes from a feeling that writers should not speak about themselves in their articles.

He liked to remain invisible all the time, but his presence was there for us to experience. Even in personal conversations, Ayyappa Paniker was not in the habit of speaking about himself. Nor did he encourage anyone if they spoke about him. As his friends and colleagues knew about his aversion

---

1 From "*Kudumbapuranam*" translated into "The Family Saga", *Selected Poems of Ayyappa Paniker* (Trivandrum: Modern Book Centre, 1985: 41).

for praise, they remained cautious. His reason for avoiding interviews was that if he agreed to them, he would have to give replies to queries about his "sacrifices", his "heroic stories", the "genesis and evolution" of his "great" works and so on, and thus speak about himself.

Isn't it a matter of honour for us that a famous person, living in times when people are besotted with themselves, did not like to talk about himself?

24
Salman Rushdie

ONE DAY IN 1988, when I was working as a guest lecturer in journalism at Madras Christian College in Chennai (before the publication of Salman Rushdie's *The Satanic Verses*) Ayyappa Paniker called to inform me that a British television company named Channel 4 was producing a television film series based on Salman Rushdie's famous novel *Midnight's Children*. The channel personnel wanted a person interested in literature and journalism to help them, from writing the script right up to the shoot. Ayyappa Paniker wanted to know whether I was interested in the project.

Who would let go of an invaluable opportunity to interact with a world-renowned novelist like Rushdie? Without asking any questions, I jumped at the offer. The novel that had earned its author the Booker Prize and Booker of Bookers Prize told the tales of children believed to be born at the midnight hour of 14 August 1947, when India gained freedom, as well as the story of post-independence India. As I worked on the project of the television series planned on this novel, I realised that the remuneration and other allowances were very generous.

The Foreword newly written for the latest edition of *Midnight's Children* which carried Rushdie's critique of Indira Gandhi and the Emergency had kicked up quite a storm in Bombay, the author's place of birth, as well as in many other parts of India. (That India was the first country to ban *The Satanic Verses* was not entirely accidental.) Therefore, all the work on the film was done in secret. Special instructions were given to ensure that information about the project did not get leaked to the press.

Rushdie came to Kerala more than once. I could drive him to several places and organise the shoots—this opportunity to interact with a world-renowned writer was made possible by Ayyappa Paniker.

***

My son Gautam had just completed his 12th standard exams. One evening, I went to Ayyappa Paniker's house along with him and Jessy. Ayyappa Paniker asked Gautam what he was reading just then. He replied that it was *Ulysses*, and added that going through the novel was very laborious. Ayyappa Paniker suggested that he read Homer's *Iliad* and James Joyce's *A Portrait of the Artist as a Young Man* so that *Ulysses* would make sense more easily. Both books were bought in a couple of days. A little later, Gautam received an interview call for admission to the BA course in English language and literature at St Stephen's, Delhi, and he left soon thereafter.

At the interview, Gautam faced the same question ("What are you reading these days?"). "*Ulysses,*" he replied.

"How is it?" was the next query.

Gautam said he was finding it difficult to continue reading the book. The next question was why he was making that much effort. He stated that he was determined to read it to the end because one of his teachers had said, "It is the most talked about book but the least read one." When a teacher in the panel advised Gautam to read Homer's *Iliad* and James Joyce's *A Portrait of the Artist as a Young Man* so that *Ulysses* would become more accessible, Gautam replied that he had already read them. The interview then began to focus on those books and on reading in general.

I believe that Gautam gained entry into St Stephen's because of the intellectual intervention of Ayyappa Paniker, even without Gautam being aware of it.

***

As a young poet and student at the Institute of English, Atmaraman did not have a great opinion about Ayyappa Paniker the poet. But Ayyappa Paniker did not take it seriously at all. In fact, he encouraged Atmaraman to write poems and critical articles. In due course of time, Atmaraman landed a job, and had to undergo a seven months of training in Bombay. Before he left, he visited Ayyappa Paniker for the sake of formality. Atmaraman himself has recorded the "small, big thing" that happened that day:

> When I went to take leave, Ayyappa Paniker—without my asking—handed over an envelope and said, "This is a letter to my friend in Bombay. Go to him if you have any need. Before you leave Bombay, I'll come there some day." I turned, walked some distance, and only then did I notice the address on the envelope. It was Professor Nissim Ezekiel! (*Bhashaposhini*, 2006 October: 33).

Nissim Ezekiel, the most influential, respected and noteworthy among the poets of post-independence India, who was born and raised in Bombay!

Did Atmaraman stand there incredulous and dumbfounded that day? Yes, I imagine he did.

***

How do you slot an individual with such a distinctive personality? As a poet? Translator? Critic? Prose writer? Scholar? Editor? Organiser? Teacher? Or, someone higher?

It is virtuous indeed to remain honest, and live one's life without causing harm to anyone. But isn't it nobler still to do one's best for the progress of others, that too, without a thought about getting anything in return?

25
Who is This Man?

IN 2002, DURING my days in the ICU of the Medical College Hospital in Kottayam, after I was involved in a car crash, my wife Jessy kept consoling me by saying that friends, who I was confident would stand by me in times of crisis, were indeed enquiring and feeling anxious about me. Among the names she mentioned was Ayyappa Paniker's. Jessy even thought that the reason for the extraordinarily warm attitude shown by the doctors, nurses and others in the hospital was the sheer number of calls that came from various places, asking how I was. The words of Dr Dayanand Babu, professor and head of the Department of Surgery, who stood strongly by me both during my ICU stay and my subsequent period of convalescence, remain in my memory even today.

Ayyappa Paniker was the chief guest at an annual function of Medical College, Kottayam. Dr Dayanand Babu was seated next to him. In a bid to bridge the gap of unfamiliarity between them, Dr Dayanand told Ayyappa Paniker, who used to call the principal of the college to learn details about my health condition:

> "When Priyadas was in Medical College after the accident, I was in charge of his treatment." In sheer gratitude, Ayyappa Paniker held both my hands and remained silent for a few moments, and when he stood up to express his thankfulness, both of us became emotional.

***

I got a further glimpse of Ayyappa Paniker's love and concern for me on another occasion in a different way. I regained my health and returned to normal life only after spending several months at Medical College, Kottayam, the KIMS Hospital in Thiruvananthapuram and at home. Although there were responsible people supervising my business matters on a day-to-day basis, Jessy very meticulously took many decisions, looked after our school-going son, and welcomed as well as accommodated guests in accordance with their wishes. Ayyappa Paniker who used to come to our house frequently during this period observed all this keenly. After I regained my health, one day when Ayyappa Paniker paid us a visit, he said to me, "You should not do anything in life that will cause pain to Jessy, okay?" As a result, even today, whenever any disagreement begins to rear its head between us, Jessy gleefully reminds me, "Don't forget what Paniker sir told you!"

***

Let me quote Vinaya Kumar, who worked as a teacher at several government colleges in Kerala:

> In personal relationships, he had compassion and consideration for others. Whenever I think of him, an incident comes to mind. When the father of one of his students passed away, Ayyappa Paniker sir went to the student's house to see him on that night of heavy rain, and waited at the threshold for nearly an hour (*Ayyappa Paniker Forever*, Folio, 2019: 64).

***

Let me share another anecdote. It was narrated by Dr Tommy John, one of Ayyappa Paniker's students. Tommy John wanted to join the Institute of English to do his MA in English under Ayyappa Paniker, who was the Head of the Department (HoD), but the first call letter for admission to the MA course came from Fatima Mata National (FMN) College, Kollam. A week after he gained admission there, he received a letter from the Institute of English, directing him to be present at the Institute with all the relevant documents. Tommy reached the Institute at the appointed hour, along with his father. As he was not very sure of securing admission there, he had not cancelled his admission at FMN College or retrieved the required documents. When he entered Ayyappa Paniker's room, he showed the call letter, but Ayyappa Paniker asked for the relevant certificates. When Tommy said that he did not have them with him, Ayyappa Paniker's tone became harsh. He sent Tommy back with the instruction that if he wanted admission to the Institute, he had to come back with the certificates.

As Tommy stepped out, crestfallen, his father asked him, "Do you want admission to this institution itself?" but finally yielded to his son's insistence.

Both of them quickly boarded a bus to Kollam. By afternoon, they reached FMN College and met the principal to tell him about the problem. He was willing to ask the college office to return the documents to Tommy, but admissions were about to be closed that day and all the students' certificates sent to the university immediately. Therefore, if Tommy did not secure admission to the Institute of English, he would not be able to gain re-entry into FMN College. On hearing this piece of information, Tommy and his father realised the risk involved in the decision.

Tommy's father tried to dissuade his son from taking back the certificates but Tommy stood firm. Eventually, after collecting them, they took a train to Thiruvananthapuram at 2.30 in the afternoon. The train would reach its destination at 4 p.m., which left them enough time to reach the Institute office before it closed at 5 in the evening. But, quite unexpectedly, the train stopped at Chirayinkeezh, and remained there. Tommy's and his father's hearts throbbed faster with mounting anxiety as they sat inside the unmoving train. Eventually, an hour later, the train restarted and reached Thiruvananthapuram at 5.30 p.m., more than one-and-a-half hours after the scheduled arrival time. Although Tommy's father did not see any point in going to the university, Tommy pleaded that they hire a taxi, and try their luck.

"You'll be content only if you waste more money, isn't it?" Tommy's father seemed to say, but he agreed to the demand.

When the taxi pulled up at the portico of the Institute, not a single person was in sight anywhere. Seeing the anger and disappointment on his father's face, Tommy said, "Since we've come this far, let us go upstairs and check, before we return, Dad." He climbed up the steps, walked to the end of the veranda to find out whether the door to the HoD's room was closed. The half-doors were closed as usual, but as Tommy walked closer to the room, he heard Ayyappa Paniker's voice, "Come in!" Tommy rushed in. Collecting all the certificates from him, Ayyappa Paniker said, "I knew, Tommy, that you would come, however late it was!"

"Who is this man? What should I call him?" Tommy asked himself.

***

In 1999, V.K. Unnikrishnan, one of the editors of *Sankramanam*, died of cancer. One day, while he was undergoing treatment at the Regional Cancer Centre at Thiruvananthapuram and was in great pain, Ayyappa Paniker went to the hospital. He enquired about Unnikrishnan's condition, and sitting on a chair, recited *Gotrayanam* ("Southbound"). Hearing the lines, Unnikrishnan's face and mind became very calm. I recall that sight even today. As I stood there listening to Ayyappa Paniker's consoling lines of intensity and compassion, I realised that even the biggest catastrophes have to be faced with courage, not fear.

> With my hand on your head, I bless you.
> Stroking your forehead, I bless you.
> Touching your long eyebrows, I bless you.

Looking into your blue eyes, I bless you.
Closing your eyelids, I bless you.
My hand patting your eyelashes, I bless you.
Kissing your golden cheeks, I bless you.
With a kiss on your red lips, I bless you.
Hugging your full bosom, I bless you.
Putting a garland on your neck, I bless you.
Stroking your lovely tresses, I bless you.
Embracing your fragrant body, I bless you.
Pressing my face on your soft belly, I bless you.
Holding your whole body close, I bless you.
Seeing your twin thighs, I bless you.
Remembering their joints, I bless you.
My hands clasping your hands, I bless you.
Stroking your feet again and again, I bless you (trans. Chitra Panicker, *Samyukta* [January 2007], VII, 1: 186).

26
The Prompter, Promoter and Witness

T.P. RAJEEVAN, one of the prominent poets of the generation that followed Ayyappa Paniker's, said:

> Everybody associated with Malayalam will have an Ayyappa Paniker-experience—maybe of an alternate word suggested by him, of tidying up of a translated piece, or of being accompanied to the space beyond Malayalam literature. More than this, anyone acquainted with him will treasure at least one Ayyappa Paniker-experience in their memory—of humour-laced small talk he made, of a conversational segment that became a turning point in one's life, of a suggestion that prompted rethinking, or of a conversation that inspired an overhaul (*Bhashaposhini*, 2006 October: 29).

Not only those associated with Malayalam, but anyone who has interacted with him will have had an Ayyappa

Paniker-experience to talk about. One of the greatest actors in the field of Indian cinema, Kamal Haasan has mentioned the impact that some of Ayyappa Paniker's poems had on him. The poem Kamal Haasan wrote titled "*Sakshibhootham*" ("The Witnessing Self")—a few lines of which are quoted here—reveal how deep his Ayyappa Paniker-experience was. He was introduced to Ayyappa Paniker's poems through Neela Padmanabhan's[1] translations. In the poem, Kamal Haasan spells out his gratitude to the translator too. (The translation won the Central Sahitya Akademi Award in 2003.)

"*Sakshibhootham*"

A single line by a great poet
creates many poets.
A poem [of mine] came like that –
titled "*Sakshibhootham*".

I understand Malayalam only through the ear.
Thank you, Neela Padmanabhan,
for bringing Paniker poems
to Tamil, without dropping
their Malayalam flavour (*Mathrubhumi* weekly, 15–21 November 2020).

Ayyappa Paniker interacted with people from all walks of life, cutting across differences in status. From people like Vasu Pillai, the taxi driver, and Raghavan, a Class IV

---

1 Neela Padmanabhan (b. 1938) is an author who has composed several novels, short stories, poems and articles in Tamil and Malayalam. He writes in English too, and is a translator.

employee, to Indian Administrative Service (IAS) officers—all have experienced the generosity and inspirational power of his friendship.

Vasu Pillai, who drove his own taxi, was Ayyappa Paniker's regular driver, and drew a satisfactory and regular income from this job. Raghavan, a Class IV employee at the Institute of English, ran small errands for Ayyappa Paniker, such as purchasing books or posting letters as he went out on his regular round of duties. Whenever Raghavan ran into financial difficulties, Ayyappa Paniker extended all possible help, without any hesitation or without being told about it. Every member of the Institute staff was aware of it. T.P. Sreenivasan, former ambassador, G. Krishnan, former chief secretary, Lizzie Jacob and other IAS officers like Sajan Peter, Rajeev Sadanandan and others recall how Ayyappa Paniker awakened them with the light of his creative insights. Lizzie Jacob wrote in *Kerala Kavitha*, 2007:

> Paniker sir was my *guru*. I did not learn from him formally. He did not impart information to me inside the classroom. Rather, it was through his life that he taught me. He influenced me through his words and actions, even without my being aware of it. The impact was not in the form of creative awakening alone. It was strong enough to make elevation of personal life blessed too (219).

When the journalist Jose Panachippuram was an MA student, much of his time was taken up with treatment and injections following a dog bite during his study leave. He called up his teacher, Ayyappa Paniker and informed him that he did not plan to take his final year exams as his health was not good enough. Panachippuram recalls how Ayyappa Paniker consoled him saying that he would pass his examination with whatever he had learnt, and so there was no need to worry. The strength lent by those words was what impelled Panachippuram to take the exams and earn creditable marks.

Jojo, the investigative journalist with *Kerala Kaumudi*, remembers how Ayyappa Paniker used to call and congratulate him whenever his reports exposing cases of corruption got published. Besides Jose Panachippuram and B.C. Jojo, other journalists, such as P. Ravindran Nayar, N.R.S. Babu, Mangad Ratnakaran, Alakananda (*Asianet*), Thomas Jacob (*The Hindu*), Amrit Lal (*The Indian Express*) and others have had their Ayyappa Paniker-experiences.

Ayyappa Paniker entrusted Adoor Gopalakrishnan with the responsibility of directing the theatrical presentation of Kadammanitta Ramakrishnan's Malayalam translation of Samuel Beckett's *Waiting for Godot*. The play was successfully staged in front of a full audience at the Hassan Marikar Hall in Thiruvananthapuram. In *Kerala Kavitha*, 2007, Adoor Gopalakrishnan wrote: "When that day's presentation created waves, Paniker sir did not tell anyone that he was the master brain and master director of the entire project." The friendship between Ayyappa Paniker and Govindan Aravindan began at University College, Thiruvananthapuram, when the latter was a student there. Constant interaction with Ayyappa Paniker contributed hugely towards fashioning an exceptional film director out of Aravindan.

C.N. Sreekantan Nair's *Lanka Lakshmi* is a very difficult play to present on stage. On the occasion of C.N.'s death anniversary, it was Ayyappa Paniker who asked the actor Murali to play the role of Ravana. Murali took on the challenge and acted his part to perfection. Impressed by his performance, Ayyappa Paniker and others complimented him wholeheartedly. Later Murali said, "I place Paniker sir's evaluation much higher than all the rest I received. Had it not been for his prompting, I would not have ventured into it."

During the course of private conversations, other actors like (Bharat) Gopi, Nedumudi Venu, K.S. Gopalakrishnan, M.V. Gopakumar, Aliyar and others have also spoken proudly about the encouragement they received from Ayyappa Paniker.

Margi Madhu, a Koodiyattam performer (Koodiyattam is a theatrical art form of Kerala), states that Ayyappa Paniker was the most prominent among the scholars who went regularly to Appukuttan Nair's "Margi" at Valiyashala in Thiruvananthapuram, and offered the actors the support they deserved.

> Every week, whenever he came to see a Koodiyattam recital at "Margi", he doffed his poet-apparel, watched the performance as a mere spectator, and shared his ideas about Koodiyattam and acting, without a trace of artifice (*Bhashaposhini*, 2006 October: 43).

Ayyappa Paniker knew the most crucial aspects of the classical art forms of Kathakali and Koodiyattam, and was ever ready to nourish them.

Kanayi Kunhiraman becomes eloquent when he talks about the encouragement he received from Ayyappa Paniker not only in the field of painting but poetry as well. When Suresh Kurup (who became a Member of the Legislative Assembly [MLA] and Member of Parliament [MP]) was the chairman of the Kerala University Union during his student days, he conducted literary camps with the help of Ayyappa Paniker. M.A. Baby remembers going to meet Ayyappa Paniker before taking charge as the minister for education and culture, after being elected as an MLA. The late G. Karthikeyan (former minister) and Palode Ravi (former MLA) were also members of Paniker's circle of friends.

Ayyappa Paniker had good relations with writers in other languages in India like Nakulan (T.K. Doraiswamy) and Neela Padmanabhan in Tamil; the famous U.R. Anantamurthy, P. Lankesh, Chandrasekhara Kambar, A.K. Ramanujam and Chandrakant Deivathale in Kannada; Dilip Chitre in Marathi; Sitakant Mahapatre in Hindi and others. Many people know that Ayyappa Paniker played an important role in bringing Dr U.R. Ananthamurthy to Kerala to become the vice chancellor of MG University.

Neela Padmanabhan, who translated many of Ayyappa Paniker's poems into Tamil, highlights another facet of his personality by stating that Ayyappa Paniker saw humans as his medium. He had litterateur friends in Tamil Nadu like Ka Naa Subramanyam, Na Pichamoorthy, Si Su Chellappa, Ma Ilaya Perumal and others.

When he (Ayyappa Paniker) went to Chennai, he visited Chellappa who was ailing, and bought the novel he had written. Later he arranged a translation of one of the chapters of Chellappa's novel as well as a critical article on the novel, and got them published in *Kala Kaumudi*. Chellappa later gratefully admitted that Ayyappa Paniker's was the first gesture of recognition he received on writing that novel, and this factor paved the way for his becoming respected among the Tamil media circles.

Neela Padmanabhan mentions the indebtedness of Paul Zachariah, the noted Malayalam short story writer, to Ayyappa Paniker thus:

> "I owe a special thanks to sir [Ayyappa Paniker]. In the beginning of the 1970s, when I met sir at O.V. Vijayan's house (or his studio), I was a fledgling writer craving for attention. Sir translated a story of mine into English and published it. That was the first translation of my work" (As mentioned by Neela Padmanabhan in *Kerala Kavitha*, 2007: 225).

To substantiate his point that Ayyappa Paniker saw humans as his medium, Neela Padmanabhan quotes two anecdotes. One relates to Chellappa (whose experience is presented in the third person). The other, to Paul Zachariah (whom Neela Padmanabhan quotes). This reveals how well Ayyappa Paniker, the householder, took care of each and every flower in the garden of literature.

Hundreds of teachers—like Jancy James, Jameela Begum, Narayana Chandran, C.R. Prasad, Dominic Kattoor, Krishna Kumar, P. Radhika, Nisha Venugopal, Anjana Shankar and others—can hardly exhaust their stock of experiences of how Ayyappa Paniker was a powerhouse of ideas when they were engaged in research. They speak eloquently about his ways of inspiring and promoting them, and also about the evenings of friendly conversations with him.

In my conversations with B.C. Jojo, the topic of Ayyappa Paniker often came up for discussion. Once Jojo said, "The world imagines that poetry was Ayyappa Paniker's medium, doesn't it? But it's not poetry."

I thought about it. What could it be? What other literary genre was his medium?

Jojo began to dismiss my replies emphatically. "No, no! It's not any genre of literature."

Eventually, he told me, "Ayyappa Paniker's medium was the human being."

"But isn't that true of every writer?" I asked.

"It is. But Ayyappa Paniker's perspective was different. Human issues were the theme in his works but Ayyappa Paniker intervened in human lives too, with or without their knowledge. That was what Paniker sir did. Paniker sir could see everything only through the human medium. As a result, he entered each human, identified his/her special inner powers, and composed unique wake-up calls for them. He encouraged them to reach the heights they desired and even beyond. But this happened only to those who went close to him. He saw the world only through the lens of the human. Those who absorbed the energy he emitted and worked accordingly, as well as those who followed his instructions and optimised their talents, raised their level to the fullest extent possible. One's level may not improve all the time but the awareness that sir is beside you is a source of tremendous strength."

Maybe that was why on hearing about Ayyappa Paniker's death, Abraham Konnakkuzhi (director, H&C Books, Thrissur) lamented, "I have been orphaned…"

27
Pinnem Chankaran...[1]

I HAVE NEVER heard Ayyappa Paniker belittle anyone with whom he interacted in his daily life, cultural activities or workplace, either in his speeches or in his writings. As a critic, he has commented on the works of Vallathol Narayana Menon, Joseph Mundassery, N.V. Krishna Warrier and others, but even his references to certain vices or people who were

---

1 Part of a Malayalam idiom *"Pinnem chankaran thengel thanne"* ("Again, Chankaran is on the coconut palm") that is roughly equivalent to "back to square one". Chankaran is depicted as a country lout. Metaphorically, he is a stick-in-the-mud, who does not change his stance, whatever happens. "Chankaran" is a corrupt form of "Sankaran". Ayyappa Paniker uses this idiom to tease Thayat Sankaran whose obstinacy, as revealed in his book *Adhunika Kavithayude Jeerna Mukham* (The Decayed Face of Modernist Poetry), is not very dissimilar to that of his arboreal counterpart!

enslaved to them were rendered in a mild language and tone. It is true that he wrote humorous lines that carried satiric resonances. Maybe he believed that no one had the right to fault others. Yet he never conveyed such a message through his speeches, prose writings, poems or in his conversations. Criticisms were always mild, although his humour was sharp.

When Ayyappa Paniker sent his poem "*Mrityupuja*" ("Hymn to Death") to a weekly, the scholarly editor changed the first line from "*Mandagamini, hemanthayamini*" ("Slow-moving winter night") to "*He mandagamini, hemanthayamini*" ("O slow-moving winter night"). Ayyappa Paniker did not like the editorial change at all, but he did not raise a complaint or protest. However, when the editor sought his photograph to publish along with the poem, Ayyappa Paniker sent it but added a note conveying his hope that the photograph would not be edited! This anecdote is cited by the critic Thomas Mathew in one of his articles. Hopefully, even the editor appreciated Ayyappa Paniker's very original albeit critical sense of humour!

Joseph Mundassery was one of the staunchest critics of Ayyappa Paniker, but note what Ayyappa Paniker wrote about him:

> That tusker has the grandeur and the self-confidence to stand in the front row and carry the *thidambu*.[2]

---

[2] The metal plaque that carries an embossed replica of the deity of a temple. It is mounted on an elephant and taken around the temple to the accompaniment of instrumental music, for devotees to offer worship.

Occasionally, he would go into a rut. That was but natural. Flamboyance suited that orator well, and he liked it too. Majestic language, majestic voice, majestic gestures. But the number of those who consider Mundassery's public activity as a loud spectacle, reminiscent of *Pandhavadyam* and *Pandimelam*,[3] is not insignificant. In most people's opinion, at certain times, his personal prejudices and partiality did come into play. [. . .] But on this happy occasion of his centenary, let us divert our attention from his negative aspects to his achievements (*Vyaktichitrangal, Yatradrishyangal* [Personal Profiles, Travel Sights], Cultural Publications Department, Government of Kerala, 2005: 72–74).

***

Among the poetic trinity—Vallathol Narayana Menon, Kumaran Asan and Ulloor S. Parameswara Iyer—Ayyappa Paniker liked Asan the best. Ulloor came next. But even when he criticised Vallathol, the decorum he showed was unparalleled:

> It is not right to decide the greatness of a poet merely on the strength of factors that attracted the readers. It will be noticed that many of Vallathol's works—which Vallathol critics, especially the admiring class, consider as his greatest achievements—have lost some of their value due to passage of time and change in taste. Take, for instance, Vallathol's political poems. One will see

---

3 Musical ensemble, using percussion instruments, cymbals and horns, played in association with temple festivals.

subjects, like Gandhi, charkha, satyagraha, anti-British sentiments and so on, tangled in works, that are nothing but speeches converted into poems. In fact, there is a significant number of works which provoke the feeling that he did not have a strong emotional involvement in certain subjects such as those. One may not see many poems that completely avoid plain declarations and announcements (*Ayyappa Panikerude Lekhanangal: 1980–90* [Ayyappa Paniker's Prose Writings: 1980–90], DC Books, 1990: 257).

This soft approach in his criticism of Vallathol is Ayyappa Paniker's natural style. It is a similar, non-condemnatory method he adopted when he established that the works of N.V. Krishna Warrier, who began writing poetry in a manner utterly different from the poems of Changampuzha Krishna Pillai, the renowned poet of Kerala, lost their flow and beauty when Warrier made his poems prose-like with his exhibition of scholarship and discursive styles.

Warrier's poetry is a proclamation of liberation from Changampuzhaism. It is a rough by-lane towards new poetry. But the presentation of emotions needs to be richer. Has his scholarship become an obstacle in its path? With excessive description and narration of the peculiar features of incidents and objects, Warrier's poetry sometimes loses its rhythm and proportion, and becomes uncomely (*Ayyappa Panikerude Lekhanangal, 1950–80* [Ayyappa Paniker's Prose Writings, 1950–80], DC Books, 1985: 26).

***

Thayat Sankaran launched an attack on Ayyappa Paniker through his book *Adhunika Kavithayude Jeerna Mukham* (The Decayed Face of Modernist Poetry), but Ayyappa Paniker did not criticise him in retaliation. Instead, he penned a reply in the form of a poem:

> The pennant's hoisted at Ayyappan kavu,
> Again, Chankaran is on the coconut palm.
> The festival at Allimalarkavu is over,
> Again, Chankaran is on the coconut palm.
> ....
> Chankaran of that place has not climbed down,
> Nangeli! Sister-in-law! Please be quick, come!
> All the coconut palms have slumped to the ground,
> Again, Chankaran is on the coconut palm. ("*Pinnem Chankaran*" ["Again, Chankaran"])

As Thayat Sankaran refused to change according to the times, even those who belonged to the movement of which he was a part, refused either to acknowledge his obstinate viewpoint or promote his book in any way, and maintained their distance from such a literary stand.

Not only did Ayyappa Paniker not criticise his detractors but he even treated them with democratic respect, and cooperated with them. What is said of Sree Narayana Guru (the spiritual leader, social reformer and philosopher)—he never spoke disrespectfully about anyone—holds true of Ayyappa Paniker also.

28
The Iconoclastic Model

A model that ought not to be followed is the perception that the composition of poetry is a strenuous penance—and as far as Ayyappa Paniker is concerned, there are no inviolable rules in poetry-writing. Rather, it is an art form which permits anything. At one point of time, he writes love poems and at another, ridicules them. Then, he returns to love poem or writes on something he had ridiculed earlier. Everything is permissible to Ayyappa Paniker. Any kind of poem can be expected from him anytime. Fortunately, all new poets, except Ayyappa Paniker, have escaped falling into this treacherous trap of playfulness. No poet in our time should be like this.

THESE LINES ARE adapted from an article titled "*Nammude Kavikal Ee Mattil Aavathirikkatte*" ("May our poets not be like this") written by K.C.

Narayanan, a literary observer, journalist and writer. It appeared in the magazine *Jwala* in 1983. He was a senior journalist, who took a keen interest in happenings in the fields of literature and culture, and had many years of professional experience with *Mathrubhumi* and *Malayala Manorama*, two of the most popular Malayalam dailies in Kerala. When I met him in 2016, these were the reasons why I alluded to his 1983 article and asked him whether he would be interested in participating in a seminar planned by the Ayyappa Paniker Foundation. The seminar would be on "Ayyappa Paniker: Agreements and Disagreements", and I suggested that K.C. Narayanan should present a paper on his disagreements with Ayyappa Paniker. His reply was somewhat on these lines:

> A few days after that article was published, I got a letter from Paniker sir. As a fellow-traveller of Modernism, I had used harsh language to criticise Ayyappa Paniker whom literary aesthetes had admiringly labelled as the Master of Modernism. So, I reckoned my criticism would have certainly injured him, and therefore, it may be a letter conveying his pain and protest in refined language. But when I broke open the letter, what I saw was the exact opposite. It seems Paniker sir was in full agreement with my observations! Over and above it, he conveyed his deep gratitude for them!

We laughed over this anecdote, and as we parted, K.C. Narayanan stated that he was involved in rereading Ayyappa Paniker's works and giving serious thought to their import.

Therefore, his request was that I should not compel him to present a paper at the seminar.

In 2022, I contacted him once again. I told him that the Foundation was planning to publish a book on the impact of Ayyappa Paniker on Malayalam literature. I needed Narayanan's permission to compose a detailed response to his earlier article, but he told me that a reply was not necessary at all because he had since then undertaken a profound study of Ayyappa Paniker, and revised his opinion. In fact, a book based on his altered perspective was on the anvil!

Thus, as we study Ayyappa Paniker in greater depth, we begin to wonder whether he is an iconoclastic model, a sublime model, a mere model or even an unexemplary one!

***

In 1973, when Ayyappa Paniker was made a reader of English at the Institute, Dr N.A. Kareem, a fellow contender to the post who had lost out in the race, filed a case in the High Court, challenging the decision of the University of Kerala. The registrar of the university, Professor A. Sreedhara Menon, would later write about this incident in the *Mathrubhumi* weekly. A few sentences from it will suffice to throw light on Ayyappa Paniker's personality.

> I had known Ayyappa Paniker since the time I was a student at the University College. A peculiarity of his that commanded my respect, during the time of the legal case against him, was the sheer indifference he showed. In the usual run of things, on such occasions, most teachers would keep in constant touch with the

officers at the university in order to learn about the twists and turns of the case. Ayyappa Paniker was an exception to this norm. He never pretended that he was a big intellectual or a cultural leader. Humility was the hallmark of his nature. A small-built man with absolutely no intellectual arrogance – a colossus! (*Mathrubhumi* weekly, 2006 September: 4).

What happened subsequently was this. The court pronounced that the appointment of Ayyappa Paniker was right. However, Ayyappa Paniker's opinion was that Dr Kareem too should be made a reader. Time passed, and Dr Kareem became the pro vice chancellor of the University of Calicut. I assumed there was every possibility that the two individuals would have drifted apart, and on making enquiries, I chanced upon a few lines penned by Dr Kareem himself in 1990 about Ayyappa Paniker. Their friendship had not suffered any dent. "If there was any suspicion of a damage, Ayyappa Paniker himself took the initiative to repair it. That nice gentleman never showed any unnecessary obstinacy or enmity in such matters."

The bond of friendship continued until Ayyappa Paniker's death. None of Ayyappa Paniker's colleagues or other teacher-friends were ever jealous of him because of the deep love and respect he commanded among students. Rather, their own respect for him grew on seeing it. Dr Kareem continues:

> Paniker has a vast circle of students. Many of them occupy high positions in life. But the love and respect they show towards Paniker strike me with wonder.

The humility and respect they show towards this small man is eloquent evidence of how deeply his personality as a teacher has impacted them (*Ayyappa Paniker: Vyakthiyum Kaviyum* [Ayyappa Paniker: The Individual and the Poet], DC Books, 1990: 40).

Who was that physically small but intellectually big man with no saintly pretensions who yet lived as the most ordinary person among ordinary people, and departed leaving a trail of light behind him?

29
Seeing One's Pupil as a Teacher

JUST BECAUSE AYYAPPA Paniker conducted himself as an ordinary teacher, people never recognised the *sanyasi* in him. He lived like a cultural *sanyasi*, without any religious trappings. As his conversations did not carry any spiritual overtones, the ascetic in him was almost unnoticed. Being a witness, being involved, yet becoming invisible in the process—that was Ayyappa Paniker's style. He never showed any interest in social positions or any desire for money and humbly rejected many positions that were offered to him. Whatever salary he received, gave him satisfaction. He did not want more.

Although he was a guide and source of support to many colleagues, co-writers, up-and-coming poets and students, he did not show special closeness to any single individual although many imagined that he had a particular fondness for them.

Ayyappa Paniker did not have complaints about anyone or anything. He took on the duty of redressing complaints through his life and his works. His *Gopikadandakam* ("The Song of the Cowherdess") was a rejoinder to Sugathakumari's *Krishna nee enne ariyilla* ("Krishna, you don't know me ..."), and it has the power to transcend time and cross geographic boundaries. Very close friends have testified that he survived the sorrows of his personal life with the stoicism of an ascetic.

The distinctive feature of Ayyappa Paniker's personality was that it completely eschewed showiness. We live amidst people who exhibit more than they have. But Ayyappa Paniker presented only as much of his vast scholarship as the occasion warranted or the forum demanded. It was only when he participated in an international seminar, as a representative of the country or of Malayalam, that others came to fathom the sheer depth of his erudition.

T.N. Jayachandran, IAS, wrote in *Kerala Kavitha* 2007 about his teacher Ayyappa Paniker thus:

> Ayyappa Paniker taught me English. But what I learnt from him was not only English. In humility, simplicity, firmness of opinion, courage and many other exemplary qualities, he was a model (172).

Rhetorical flourishes and high oratory were not his forte. Neither his lips nor his pen would allow words to be uttered or written in an irresponsible fashion or to make an impression. In fact, most of the time, he did not even use as many words as were required, preferring instead to let his listeners exercise their freedom to either finish his sentences or guess their import. Sometimes conversations would stop midway, with humour or a significant expression completing his point. Maybe that was why he wrote poems that were merely two, four or five lines long.

"*Guru*"

He who sees a pupil as *guru*
Is the greatest of all *guru*s.

No one could ever spot artificiality in any of his actions. In his poems, he made abundant use of paradox, irony, self-mockery, satire as well as pure humour and black humour—just as he did in his daily life too. But his articles and other prose pieces were simple and transparent. Ayyappa Paniker did not have the airs of a scholar, the pretence of a saint, the swagger of a simple man or the pride of a humourist. He maintained a certain distance from it all. In a sense, he transcended all these roles.

30
Personal Profiles

IN AN ATTEMPT to understand Ayyappa Paniker better, I decided to examine what he had written about himself. I did not find anything at all. He did not write an autobiography nor did he give interviews or participate in any formal discussions.

But just when I hit a road block, another path emerged in front of me. I thought that if he had written about anyone, it would invariably be equivalent to the respect he felt for them. Thus, if he showed respect to anyone, it was possible to identify the virtues he liked, and through that find out more about the value systems he cherished. It was with this intent that I went through the various personal profiles he had painted. His *Vyaktichitrangal Yatradrishyangal* (Personal Profiles, Travel Sights) is a book that briefly describes a few persons against the backdrop of the experiences he had with them. It contains nearly 30 verbal pictures. All the people he portrays in this collection were his contemporaries and were famous because they made a mark in their respective fields of activity. Ayyappa Paniker wrote about the special skills and achievements that made them unique. But their leadership qualities or unique talents were not what caught his attention. Rather, their behavioural virtues were the features that left an imprint in his mind.

Although Achutha Menon committed the unpardonable mistake of remaining the chief minister of Kerala and on the side of those who clamped the Emergency on the country, he is known as one of the best administrators the state has ever seen. The special virtues that Ayyappa Paniker saw in him were many. Through his writings, Achutha Menon exemplified the dictum that differences of opinion should be presented only through mild language. He could show affection even to those who belonged to a different party. Such a democratic respect for opposition and tolerance is very rare in politics. This essay contains the answer to the question as to why Ayyappa Paniker did not show closeness to any political party. "Maybe he [Achutha Menon] understood that in team work, certain uncontrollable failures may happen, and that theory and practice are not always good fellow-travellers" (86–88).

Ayyappa Paniker had respect for C. Unniraja because the latter remained an idealist even while he was closely associated with authority: "Even during these difficult times as ours, he could get by in life quietly, as an idealist. What would his smart friends and colleagues have thought about him for not having tried to acquire anything despite being so close to power?" (97)

Let us find out how Benedict Mar Gregorios (1916–94), metropolitan archbishop of the Syro-Malankara Catholic Church, attracted Ayyappa Paniker. "Knowledge is not a product of or power associated with intelligence alone. Love and consideration are major factors. Not hurting others is the hallmark of culture. And a cultured person is one who does not get provoked even in the face of challenges, and attempts to see both sides of a problem" (42).

Ayyappa Paniker described N.E. Balaram (1919–94), one of the founding fathers of the communist movement in Kerala who served as an MLA and MP and was a writer too, as a "scholar without an ego":

> Unostentatious clothes, egoless attitude, belief that humanism is greater than ideology—he must have imbibed all these not merely from his working-class activism in the initial years or from the fundamental principles of Gandhism but also from his awareness of the Indian tradition as well as his long exposure to literary works. He showed us that *nishkama karma* (action without any desire for its fruits) is not merely an advice put forth in the *Bhagavad Gita* but an extremely relevant concept in Left front political activism. He could also lead the life of a *karma yogi* (the righteous doer) without any religious paraphernalia (45–47).

The characteristics of A.K. Ramanujan, poet, translator and scholar, that Ayyappa Paniker identifies for special mention are some of the very qualities that Ayyappa Paniker himself tried to chisel to perfection.

> He controlled the sway of emotions with the help of his intellect. In place of a talker, he installed an orator. He reined in overdramatisation and replaced it with satire and paradox. He used sharp intellectualism, uncompromising satire and harsh language in his works. Discarding sublime style, he acknowledged everyday language as his poetic aim in order to depict quotidian life (32–34).

Have a look at the titles he chose for the articles in his book:

- Lifelong Pioneer
- Rare Selflessness
- An Aristocratic Communist
- The Youthful Ninan
- A New Model for Writing the Autobiography
- Felicitous Smile
- Fragrant Memory
- Admiration and Affection
- Pure Beauty in Cinema
- The Soft Face of Revolutionary Fervour
- Epitome of Equanimity
- Mild, Peaceful and Clear: But I shouldn't fault him!
- A Live Stream that has Ceased

- The Eternal Originality of Traditional Arts
- *Abhishekamangalam* (Greetings on Sighting 1,000 Full Moons)

In this book, Ayyappa Paniker used words to paint glowing profiles of individuals he knew well. Simultaneously, he wrote about people with such qualities that made them worthy of respect as personal friends. If we read the book a little more closely, we will realise he highlighted those very qualities in the individuals that he himself possessed in abundant measure.

As the Spanish proverb goes: "Show me who your friends are, and I'll tell you who you are".

31
Interiorisation

AYYAPPA PANIKER'S PERSONAL life and writings reveal that he considered personal and literary lives to be one whole. In an article titled *"Guruvinte Guruthwam"*, he wrote about Sree Narayana Guru thus: ". . . through his life he showed us an example of decreasing the distance between words and actions: he interiorised principles, transforming them into practice" (*Ayyappa Panikerude Lekhanangal: 1990–2005* [Ayyappa Paniker's Prose Writings: 1990–2005], DC Books, 2006: 297).

Don't these words—by highlighting the *guru*'s practical idea—strongly inspire each of us too to live in a similar manner? The reason for saying this is simple. Virtually everyone who knew Ayyappa Paniker at close quarters has testified in their own way and style, but with absolute conviction, that Ayyappa Paniker himself lived in that spirit although he never made such claims for himself. But he promised that if he got another birth, he would certainly try to lead a better life:

> Who knows perhaps
> Given another chance
> He might do a better job of it than before ("Epitaph", *Selected Poems of Ayyappa Paniker*, Modern Book Centre, 1985: 56).

Mahatma Gandhi has said, "My life is my message." Looking at Ayyappa Paniker from such a perspective, one can say that he was a true Gandhian. Whatever he believed in, he conveyed not through his words alone but through his life. Let us examine how he put into practice whatever he said and wrote in his field of literary work:

> Ezra Pound and D.H. Lawrence acknowledged the idea that correct form and metre alone did not make poetry, and that all it required was rhythm and cadence that agreed with the emotion. (How good it would be if poets in Malayalam also discarded the prescribed rules about metre and showed interest in composing poetry according to rhythm.) Eliot has said that only he who can create a rhythm of his own can be a poet (*Ayyappa Panikerude Lekhanangal: 1950–80* [Ayyappa Paniker's Prose Writings: 1950–80], DC Books, 1985: 30).

"*Ente Bhithimel*" ["Upon My Walls"], written in 1952, is the poem that is presented as his first in all the anthologies that have been published to date. However, Ayyappa Paniker published poems in a few weeklies from 1946 to 1952. In fact, in 1947, that is, in his 17th year, a collection of poems titled *Panineerpoovu* (The Rose) was published. Most of the poems in it were written in the Malayalam metres of *Keka*, *Kaakali* and *Oonakaakali*. But I have not heard Ayyappa Paniker refer to those poems written before "*Ente Bhithimel*" even in his private conversations. What this means is that the poetic canon of Ayyappa Paniker, the mature poet, began to form only with the composition of "*Ente Bhithimel*," when he ignored the poetic metres and tones of his Romantic predecessors, discarded their sweet and dulcet vocabulary, and started writing poems in rhythms he himself created.

It is in this context that the statement made earlier—that it was time poets in Malayalam discarded the prescribed rules about metre, and composed poems independently according to the rhythm—takes on a different meaning and points to a conscious decision he took to implement in his own poetic life. It appears he was very particular about first practising those very principles that he taught, believed in and popularised.

Aren't the experiments he conducted in the field of poetry proof of such a belief? If the experiments proved correct and successful, he took delight in improving and renewing them. Whatever he wanted to tell the world was conveyed through his life and his compositions. That was the reason he avoided giving interviews or making public statements. In more precise terms, Ayyappa Paniker was a practitioner who took care to decrease the gap between words and actions, and did his best to convert the two entities into one. He used his life to exemplify that what he wrote about and what he believed in were one and the same, after he had experimented with them and found them practicable.

That is why it is said that if he saw humans as his medium, he used himself first to conduct observations. Ayyappa Paniker believed that human life was about fighting problems and crises, and emerging victorious. It also meant it was only by defeating the very forces which came to defeat us, and soaring above the sky-cage, that we attained new life—and he kept refashioning his life in accordance with this belief.

32
The Solitary Tree

THERE IS ALWAYS a wireless connection between individuals who share a bond of affection that is virtually palpable when they meet, interact closely or converse. We notice this phenomenon not only among humans but in all creatures too. But Ayyappa Paniker's love was not easily detectable and hence not felt in full measure during the experience. Invariably, it was only much later that we realised that whatever he had said or done was out of love for us. And by the word "later" I mean not merely hours. In some cases, it would take days, weeks or even months for the realisation to kick in, especially since getting loved in return was not the topmost item in his list of priorities. At best, we may describe his love as other-worldly, spiritual, suprasensory or philosophical. That was the reason why many of his former students sought him out, long after they had completed their formal education under him and walked some distance on the road of life. From P. Ravindran Nayar, the translator of *Pathumanippookkal* (Poetry at Midnight) to K. Krishna Kumar, former principal of Sanatana Dharma (SD) College, Alappuzha, or from Sudha Gopalakrishnan, executive editor of Saha Media to P. Radhika of the Department of English, FMN College—the experience was the same.

Ayyappa Paniker did not think it necessary that the affection he had for anybody be conveyed to the person concerned or to any third person. While explaining the concept of the aesthetic appreciation of poetry, Ayyappa Paniker revealed his stand on love. Appreciation of poetry for him was like love or affection and as he said, "If one keeps talking about it, doubts may arise." He had no fascination for showiness and felt no need to make a display of affection to the person concerned or even speak of it to anyone else. In Western culture, it is commonplace for a man to publicly exhibit love for his wife. Ayyappa Paniker's loyalty was not to the West but to the Indian tradition.

Whether love was an innate or an acquired quality in Ayyappa Paniker is a subject that requires study. He believed that, fundamentally speaking, love should be the driving force in humans, and considered a life well lived if one prepared the right intellectual circumstances for the growth of the person one loved. That was why he never expected gratitude or even any response from anyone. This attitude could be the manifestation of the principle of *nishkama karma* (action without any desire for its fruits) mentioned in the *Bhagavad Gita* or the dictum "Don't let your left hand know what your right hand is doing" espoused by the Bible.

Love and sorrow were the two feelings that Ayyappa Paniker pursued. Yet he concealed them both and never liked to talk about them. Not only did he not promote any conversation about them, he even kept away from such topics most of the time. More often than not, we realised his love for us in his absence, in the form of memories. But those memories are heart-warming ones because by the time we became aware of them, we would have travelled far in space and time.

Ayyappa Paniker was like a person who joined us on our journey of life and became our friend, striking up a casual conversation along the way; he was like a person who not only pointed the right direction when we stood confused at a crossroads but also made sure we reached our intended destination—he was like a beacon that lit our dark path. However, when we reached our destination and turned back to convey our gratitude, he looked at us as though he did not know what had happened, and then disappeared emotionally. As we recalled all the favours he had done from the start of the journey and went back to express our thanks, we would find him cracking jokes with another person, building up a friendship, indicating the path, and accompanying him or her along the way.

Correctly identifying the skills and potential of people, awakening them even without their knowledge, making them work to the utmost so that they achieved their goals—these were what Ayyappa Paniker considered his duty to fulfil. As soon as he became familiar with anyone, he seemed determined to be of use to them, see each of them either as a member of his family, a pupil, a friend, a poet or an acquaintance. His was an ardent mind that wished the best for others, and he had an uncommon talent for awakening the latent talent in others. These were the qualities that set Ayyappa Paniker apart from the rest. As his words and his deeds were one, he wielded tremendous influence over people, even without their realizing it.

He took care to give all the support that the young writers of the new generation required and encouraged them. Although he was a *guru* to them, he behaved as though he were their friend. He invited them to present their poems at the *Sankramanam* poetry forum and published their works in *Kerala Kavitha*, thus giving a huge boost to their self-confidence. He succeeded in empowering those who attempted to pave their own path. He mingled easily with young poets in schools and colleges, joined them in teasing and laughter, and participated in their poetic forums. In the release function of *Kerala Kavitha*, he brought many such talents to the fore, and encouraged them to see their own creative abilities. That is why it is known widely that he had more poet-friends than any other poet in Kerala. He directly intervened and inspired not only poets of his own generation but the next two generations as well. After his passing, his influence on Malayalam poetry seems to glow brighter through the works of contemporary writers.

Ayyappa Paniker, who consolidated his position in the history of Malayalam literature by the 1950s, continued to be the leader of poets for nearly half a century, donning the role of a member of their family or a friend, a guide or a *guru*, without making any claims. On his death, in an article written for the *Mathrubhumi* newspaper, P.K. Rajasekharan, the critic, identified Ayyappa Paniker's significance thus:

> Whenever there was confusion, crisis or doubt, he stood like a solitary tree, his shade spreading far and wide. He was a solitary tree with many branches, towards which birds from various directions flew and perched upon for a while, and later flew away (2006: 12).

33

Awesome Paniker

IN THE COURSE of his Ayyappa Paniker Memorial Lecture, delivered online in 2021, K.G.S. observed:

> Ayyappa Paniker, this extraordinary man, cannot be confined within a specific ambit of interpretations or brought under any single label, because he is a compendium of multiple personae, diverse times, different sensibilities, many truths and varied perspectives. U.R. Ananthamurthy was a soulmate of his. Long back, when all of us were seated like this in a circle, Ananthamurthy remarked, "He is not 'Ayyappa Paniker', he is 'Awesome Paniker'!" He leaves a stamp of dignity wherever he goes, with his very simple gestures, replies, conversations and behaviour. It is hardly hyperbolic to state that Ayyappa Paniker's was a personality that had no parallels in the cultural field

of Kerala. That is because, in Malayalam, he had to his credit 16 prose works, 10 translated titles, 11 edited volumes, two anthologies of poetry containing 714 poems in all, and three collections of essays comprising 350 pieces; and in English, he authored 14 books and edited nearly 46 works, either singly or in collaboration with others.

***

When a computer programmer, an expert in web designing but a practically unlettered person in matters concerning writers and literature, was commissioned to reformat Ayyappa Paniker's official website, he saw the sheer bulk of his intellectual output and blurted in all innocence, "Didn't he have anything else to occupy him? You said he was working in a college. How then did he keep writing all the time? He too had only 24 hours in a day, after all!"

Many may find it incredible that a person could accomplish so much during his lifetime. Ayyappa Paniker worked as a committed teacher from 9 a.m. to 5 p.m. Yet, he found time for other writers and students, for participating in literary discussions, meetings and other cultural activities.

He woke up early and served tea to all the members of his family. Thereafter he prepared breakfast and lunch. After all the clearing and cleaning got done, he headed for his teaching work. On most days, he made *idli*s or *dosa*s for breakfast, along with coconut *chammanthi*[1] or *sambar* as accompanying

---

1 Usually made by grinding freshly grated coconut into a fine paste, along with green chillies, shallots, curry leaves and salt.

dishes. When many of his close friends, who were writers themselves, such as Dr M.M. Basheer, paid him an early-morning visit, they saw him making coconut *chammanthi* on the traditional grinding stone. Occasionally, in the evenings, he went to attend poets' meets or other cultural programmes, but before he left his house, he ensured that dinner had been made. On returning, he spent his time reading and writing until it was time to sleep. This was his daily routine.

Despite all these commitments, he undertook several trips within and outside India. He was a visiting professor in more than 20 foreign universities, and represented India in innumerable cultural meetings overseas. Ayyappa Paniker enjoyed warm friendships and interacted with many world writers, including Nobel Prize winners. Even amidst all these activities, he found time to be present at most family functions and festive occasions. Such a busy schedule notwithstanding, he did not use it as an excuse to turn down people when they sought appointments with him.

So, when did he find time to write so much?

There are few in the field of contemporary literature who can match Ayyappa Paniker's canon in volume, depth or diversity. More than 100 titles, either authored or edited by him in English and in Malayalam, have been published. Among them, at least six books run to nearly 1,000 pages. Isn't this creativity astounding? Isn't this quality of industriousness staggering?

Just as the IT designer had asked, we too wonder: Was his average day longer than our 24-hour span? Or, did he not sleep at all? The latter possibility seems most unlikely because as students we found him to be the most energetic among the teachers who engaged our classes. He was the most active presence during the camps and the long meetings he attended. When he was not on stage at any meeting, he was invariably the most cheerful guest, delegate, organiser or member of the audience. His presence was considered a very inspiring one at conferences that centred on academic issues.

Once, an issue of the *Sankramanam* was released at Thrissur. Ayyappa Paniker was present on the occasion along with some poets from the region. As such programmes were invariably conducted during the evening, a double room was booked for Ayyappa Paniker for the night. After the programme, as Ayyappa Paniker was about to proceed to his lodging, he asked me where my room was. Embarrassed, I had to admit that its booking had not yet been confirmed. Quick came the response, "Aren't there two beds in my room? If you don't have any other programme, you're welcome to come there." I wondered if it was discourteous to intrude into his privacy, but in my immaturity and relative ignorance of finer social etiquette, I ignored all my niggling self-doubts, and happily accompanied him. We talked about various issues, lost all sense of time, and went to bed late. However, he woke up at 5 a.m. I had heard from some senior poets that most of Ayyappa Paniker's phone calls were made at around 4.30 in the morning.

There are documents that testify that when Ayyappa Paniker took his doctoral degree from Indiana University, and later did his postdoctoral research at Yale and Harvard universities, he completed his academic responsibilities in an impeccable manner, comprehensively, correctly and well within the stipulated time frame. He also won special appreciation for this quality in these universities. It is indeed evident that he had a willingness to work hard and a flair for completing his projects perfectly and quickly. But what is truly admirable is his courageous intention to forgo rest, as well as the firmness of his mind that helped him abide by that decision till the very end of his life. He was constantly engaged in work, and shouldered heavy responsibilities all the time. But strangely, the heaviness was felt only by those who witnessed him carrying out his duties. Never did his facial expression or words convey it.

It was as though Ayyappa Paniker had made a conscious decision very early that he had to work hard throughout his life.

34
Ayyappa Paniker's Politics

AYYAPPA PANIKER, WHO caught the imagination of the young generations in the college campuses with his *Pakalukal Ratrikal* ("Days and Nights"), gave another dimension to their feelings of uneasiness with the poem titled "*Kadukka*" ("Gallnut"). To the *Sankramanam* activists who maintained an equal distance between anarchic Naxalites and hidebound communist parties while showing allegiance to the socially marginalised, Ayyappa Paniker was a very respectable figure. But he never showed either agreement or disagreement with the stances adopted by *Sankramanam*.

I don't know if there is any community of people who are as politicised as the Malayalis. Although the overbearing influence of political thinking has abated somewhat since 2000, where one's loyalties lay was a matter of considerable importance earlier. It was difficult to maintain a neutral political stand in Kerala society because adopting such a position was a choice exercised or an opinion held by individuals. Let social scientists decide whether political movements and ideologies create followers or whether individuals make their own selection. Whatever that is, the politicisation of Kerala peaked by the end of the 1960s with attacks on the Thalassery and Pulpally police stations and the martyrdom of Arikkad Varghese.[1] With the clamping of the Emergency in 1975, Kerala became totally politicised.

Ayyappa Paniker wrote very little about political leaders, and whenever he did, it was not their "heroic" deeds that he highlighted but their virtuous traits. "An Aristocratic Communist" was the phrase that Ayyappa Paniker used to describe Achutha Menon:

> I don't know whether Achutha Menon chose to contain his mental turmoil during the time of the Emergency and later during the perestroika, preferring instead to take the path of contemplation. Such a possibility cannot be disregarded (*Vyakti Chitrangal, Yatra Drishyangal* [Personal Profiles, Travel Sights], Cultural Publications Department, Government of Kerala, 2005: 86).

---

1 Arikkad Varghese (1938–70) was an idealistic comrade who chose to walk the path of Naxalism in order to fight the corrupt and exploitative feudalistic set-up and wipe out social inequality. The Naxals organised attacks on feudal lords and police stations at Thalassery, Pulpally, Thirunelli, Thrissilery and Kuttiady in Kerala. Varghese gave leadership to the riots at Thirunelli and Thrissilery, before escaping into the forests of Wayanad. He was subsequently hunted down and killed in a fake encounter.

It appears Ayyappa Paniker's respect for Achutha Menon was what made him arrive at such a justification.

Ayyappa Paniker saw N.E. Balaram as the "mild face of revolutionary fervour":

> He had the mental strength, insight and worldly wisdom to demonstrate that humility rather than cunning is a politician's asset, and also to believe as well as convince others that a politician has a mild and beautiful face (*Vyakti Chitrangal, Yatra Drishyangal* [Personal Profiles, Travel Sights], Cultural Publications Department, Government of Kerala, 2005: 45–46).

Another politician who commanded his love and respect was Unniraja because the communist leader was an idealist from the beginning to the end of his life:

> Throughout their lives, Unniraja and others believed that it was primitive to climb as much and as quickly or to amass as much as possible (*Vyakti Chitrangal, Yatra Drishyangal* [Personal Profiles, Travel Sights], Cultural Publications Department, Government of Kerala, 2005: 99).

Such assessments indicate what Ayyappa Paniker thought about the people he respected in their personal and public lives.

He acknowledged only those public activists whose actions synchronised with their words. If among public figures, only those who nurtured idealism and personal integrity commanded Ayyappa Paniker's respect, among poets, only those who embraced change and introduced novelty were selected by him for translation. It was he who gave momentum to the translation era in Malayalam poetry. He himself translated the works of Vladimir Mayakovsky, the Soviet Russian poet and playwright, Pablo Neruda, the Chilean poet and winner of the Nobel Prize for Literature in 1971, Nicolas Guillen, the Cuban poet and journalist, and others; entrusted O.N.V. Kurup with translating Spanish poet Federico Garcia Lorca; Kadammanitta with Mexican poet Octavio Paz, who won the Nobel Prize for Literature in 1990; Attoor with Soviet Russian poet and writer Andrei Voznesensky; Satchidanandan with Indonesian poet Chairil Anwar; K.G.S. with a few Kannada poets; and Deshamangalam with some Punjabi poets. What followed was a vibrant period during which all the major world poets, including German playwright Bertolt Brecht, became household names among the Malayalam reading public.

When Ayyappa Paniker translated T.S. Eliot's *The Waste Land*, he was branded as an advocate of imperialism. When he threw his weight behind individual freedom, organisations took offence. But as soon as readers and writers of the new generation all over Kerala began to align themselves with his philosophies as well as observations, and enjoy his translations, poems and articles, opposition to him gave way to acceptance. Those who had rejected him soon realised their mistake and withdrew themselves.

Nicolas, the friend of the twentieth century,
I dedicate this to you.

The anthology of Cuban poems translated by Ayyappa Paniker was dedicated to Nicolas Guillen. He formed a warm personal relationship with Guillen who was Cuban leader Fidel Castro's friend. His popular poem titled "Havana" features Cuba, Castro and Che Guevara as characters. It was Ayyappa Paniker who took the initiative to award the Asan World Prize for poetry to Guillen.

Ayyappa Paniker earned his PhD degree for his research on the poems of Robert Lowell. Could it be only a mere coincidence that Lowell was in the forefront of the agitation led by American intellectuals against the US war on Vietnam?

Ayyappa Paniker's thoughts may have been influenced by his closeness to M. Govindan who had accepted M.N. Roy's political line of radical humanism that attempted a link between liberalism and communism. His conversations and poems seem to convey his doubt as to whether politicians live according to the belief systems they hold aloft. His politics, in its most fundamental sense, encompassed humanism, an ability to empathise with suffering fellow humans, and a willingness to give them what they required instead of doling out ideologies.

Ayyappa Paniker did not think that the belief systems of a group of people could offer any assistance to those who were capable of independent thought. It was his conviction that the originality of individuals was the driving force behind the renewal of ideas and the building of a new world. He was not interested in being a part or a member of any organisation or party or being obsequious to any entity because organised institutions symbolised centralisation of authority rather than democracy.

Party politics revolves around power and authority. Ayyappa Paniker knew that power tended to corrupt people, therefore, he showed no interest in being associated with party politics.

> On merely seeing the ladder of power
> there arises a yearning to clamber ("*Adhikarasaurabhyam*" ["The Fragrance of Authority"]).

35

The Leading Light

IT MAY BE true that Ayyappa Paniker sought to encourage only those who showed some flair, interest or potential. Although he saw human beings as his medium, he could only work with those who demonstrated some level of interest, taste or talent. He could be described as a creator of perspectives, but this was possible only if he detected a glimmer of an inner spark in the individuals who approached him.

While working with people as a medium, he made no distinction based on gender. He encouraged everyone to the fullest extent of their innate ability and character and even accompanied them on their journey. Regardless of whether the path was difficult, an arduous climb, full of stones and thorns, or tediously long, he remained a constant companion.

Samyukta is an English journal on Women's Studies published from Thiruvananthapuram that gives prominence to literature and is run by a group of English teachers who are interested in English language, literature and teaching. Ayyappa Paniker not only gave it his blessings and goodwill but his wholehearted cooperation as well. His help took the form of advice and instructions as well as guidelines regarding the shaping of its content and sourcing of relevant materials. In the editorial of one of its issues, Dr G.S. Jayasree wrote:

> Supriya, Radhika, Hema, Jayasree (Ramakrishnan) and myself (members of the editorial team of *Samyukta*)— bound together by love and respect for one man— Dr K. Ayyappa Paniker. He was a poet with the wisdom of a philosopher and the charisma of a rhetorician, but to us he was teacher and mentor. He gave direction to our lives, encouraged and supported us.

Many English teachers enjoyed this kind of bond with Ayyappa Paniker. In January 2007, the *Samyukta* team brought out an exclusive issue dedicated to Ayyappa Paniker in order to show their immense gratitude to the *guru* who had helped them and contributed to their project.

During the time I was a student at the Institute of English, Ayyappa Paniker used to invite students from various colleges in the city, who were interested in writing poems in English, to meet at the Institute after 4 p.m. every Thursday. There, the youngsters recited their poems and listened to others' works. It was a huge opportunity that he opened up for the aspiring poets and he also helped them publish their works in various journals, magazines and anthologies. Although Ayyappa Paniker himself never wrote poems in English, his presence and conversations with the budding poets gave them a lot of confidence. Many poetry clubs that took birth from such meetings are active even today. Besides, he arranged opportunities for the youngsters to interact with many Indian poets in English, like Kamala Das, Dom Moraes, R. Parthasarathy and others.

Dr S. Sreenivasan, former head of the Department of English of Sree Narayana (SN) College, Kollam, brings out a journal called *Journal of Literature and Aesthetics*, which he edits. Ayyappa Paniker played the role of an adviser and collaborated with him substantially in soliciting works of writers from all over the world and inviting them to seminars. He was also instrumental in marshalling the involvement of prominent Indian poets in English, like Jayanta Mahapatra, Kamala Das, Meena Alexander and others. When the publication of the journal hit a roadblock for a brief while, Ayyappa Paniker's intervention spurred it on to new life, and this is gratefully recorded by Dr Sreenivasan himself. *Littcrit*, a biannual English journal started by Dr P.K. Rajan in 1975, was also a beneficiary of Ayyappa Paniker's intellectual support.

Similarly, Ayyappa Paniker did his best to nourish the literary taste of new generations of students writing poems in English by encouraging them to contribute to *Kavya Bharati* and *Kavithalaya*, both published by the Study Centre for Indian Literature in English and Translation (SCILET), the library in Madurai. The editor of *Kavithalaya* recalled that in a poetry workshop conducted in 1995 at the Kodaikanal International School, Ayyappa Paniker had been invited to chair the workshop but he was like one of the organisers, always approachable and sitting amidst the participants, or like a friend, initiating discussions on creative compositions.

A segment of K.G.S.'s speech, delivered online in 2021 on the occasion of the 90th birth anniversary of Ayyappa Paniker arranged by the residents of Kavalam, a village on the banks of the Vembanad lake in Alappuzha district where Ayyappa Paniker was born and brought up, is relevant in this context:

> Once, when the East-West University of the US expressed interest in publishing an anthology of Ayyappa Paniker's poems, he replied that he had a collection of poems written by other poets in his language, and suggested that they be compiled to make the volume. That is the greatness of Paniker sir. That is the thought of a truly noble individual. He brought out an anthology of poems of his time. What the university said about it later was noteworthy. "Poets from a lot of countries have come here. Whenever we showed interest in bringing out a collection of their poems, they immediately gave us their works along with their detailed biodata. But it never contained the distinctive stamp of the poetry of their land."

36
"Ayyappa Paniker is Not Profitable at all"

Only narcissists have gained many admirers in Kerala. Paniker hated self-advertisement. He indulged in self-mockery. Imitators are few and that trend is likely to continue. Ayyappa Paniker is not profitable at all (*Ayyappa Paniker: Jeevitharekha* [Ayyappa Paniker: Life Sketch], DC Books, 2007: 81).

THIS OBSERVATION BY poet and writer Kalpetta Narayanan is very significant. Positions of power and authority are necessary if we wish to satisfy our admirers. Followers will not hang around us if there are no prospects of returns. Needless to say, this matters little if we do not want people to sing hallelujahs or to organise receptions in order to boost our ego.

Ayyappa Paniker holds a pre-eminent place among the respectable people who have graced the literary and cultural spheres of Kerala. The reason for this is not difficult to find. He maintained an uncompromising distance from positions of power, privileges and fame.

Our life becomes blessed not from the wealth we amass but from the number of people we share it with (be it money, knowledge or anything else). Many publishers and editors know that over and above his teaching job, Ayyappa Paniker undertook projects for which he sought no remuneration. In fact, he worked tirelessly and without any thought about returns in order to give shape to books that would contribute to the fields of language and literature. We are already aware of the many instances when he extended financial help to those who needed it even when they did not make any explicit requests.

Although he accepted a few awards like the Kabir Samman and the Saraswathy Samman, Ayyappa Paniker kept away as far as possible from prizes and *ponnada*s.[1] When he received the Kabir Samman, his question was what *samman* might the 15th-century poet and saint Kabir himself have received! "Didn't Edappally[2] die before he won

---

1 Shawls with *zari* borders, that are wrapped around guests on ceremonial occasions as a mark of respect.

2 Edappally Raghavan Pillai (1909–36) was a contemporary of Changampuzha Krishna Pillai, who played a substantial role in ushering Romanticism into Malayalam poetry. His words include *Maninadam*, *Thusharaharam* and *Hrydayasmitham*. It is popularly believed that Changampuzha's most famous poem "Ramanan", a pastoral elegy, was written in his honour.

awards? Even Ezhuthachan[3] received no awards!"

It is common knowledge that he politely turned down many prestigious awards, and excused himself from being a member of any award committee. Only once did he become a member, and that was in order to decide the best international candidate for the Asan World Prize for poetry. Isn't it a wonder that such a person lived in this world that is constantly bombarded by news coverage of awards being presented and accepted?

Fame need not necessarily be an honest indicator of virtue. It is largely a constructed entity. Ayyappa Paniker, who firmly believed that endorsement by the crowds is not a pointer to high quality, never endeavoured to be a crowd-puller. Nor were his works designed along the lines of popular models. Most of the time, people prefer a show of numbers, size and quantity to virtue, righteousness, sterling qualities and excellence. Huge crowds may accentuate the marketability of something – politicians, religious authorities and owners of shopping malls depend on crowds, and in order to ensure continuance of their own fame, organise ostentatious wedding ceremonies, birthday parties, funeral rites and so on.

What Ayyappa Paniker said was that worshippers give importance to devotion and rituals. They do not think at all! Maybe that was why he never sought visibility; instead, he evaded attention. Most people like to be in the forefront

---

3 Thunchath Ramanujan Ezhuthachan, a Malayalam poet, translator and linguist, who lived in the 16th century. He is known as the father of modern Malayalam.

because it guarantees fame. They are obsessed with high status, the centre stage, the camera eyes focused on them, and the video angles capturing their best look. But Ayyappa Paniker was not interested in any of this. What mattered to him was achieving his aims, not eliciting applause. Instead of attempting to win others' appreciation, what he did was to give fearless expression to his original thoughts and ideas, and free rein to his imagination. That is perhaps why we sorely feel his absence even today.

Now, as I look back, I think that time has proven his wisdom right. As social creatures, we ought to adopt his method of addressing a problem according to its specific nature and finding an appropriate solution, an approach that was ridiculed in his time as apolitical because he remained equidistant from the peddlers of orthodoxy and the adherents of new ideologies. If we associate ourselves with any political movement, and when it gives birth to a government, it will require an ascetic temperament to categorically turn down the concessions, honours, positions and wealth-generating avenues that such a government offers. If we are obsequious towards any religion, we stand to gain prominence at various fora through the recommendations made by religious authorities. But Ayyappa Paniker wore the garb of an ordinary man, without any trappings of rituals or customs, and dedicated his life to selfless work like a renunciate. It does not require any special courage to be a part of the crowd, but it calls for formidable inner strength to stand alone.

Everyone knows the story of Ayyappa Paniker politely declining the offer of the post of the president of the

Kerala Sahitya Akademi. During the course of a personal conversation, the writer, editor and publisher M.R. Thampan, who accompanied the minister, G. Karthikeyan, to Ayyappa Paniker's house to request him to accept the offer, said that Ayyappa Paniker simply wanted to live life on his own terms, immersed in reading, writing and participating in cultural activities.

"*Adhikarasaurabhyam*" ("The Fragrance of Authority") is a poem that reveals his take on positions of power. When he was the head of the Institute of English, the department under the University of Kerala, the authority associated with the status never turned his head. Although colleagues and students experienced the toughness of attitude that his position demanded, the warmth that his conversations, behaviour and friendship naturally exuded remained the same.

He not only turned down the offer of the position of vice chancellor softly, but even made a joke of it saying, "I don't have so many vices!" The news of his declining the post was conveyed by the minister for education himself to M.K. Sanoo. But two days later, when Ayyappa Paniker and M.K. Sanoo met and talked over a cup of tea, Ayyappa Paniker made no mention either of his interface with the minister, the reason for their meeting or his declining the offer! K. Chandrasekharan, the minister for education, told M.K. Sanoo, then an MLA:

> One has to prostrate at Ayyappa Paniker's feet. So many people come to me with so many recommendations

in order to get the post of the vice chancellor! You too have seen such attempts. Imagine seeing a man like this amidst all of them! He said in all humility that he was content with his teaching career.

John Paul, the screenplay writer, once remarked in the programme titled "Smrithi" (Memory) telecast on Safari Channel, "Ayyappa Paniker's personality is one that has no parallels!"

37
Poetry at Midnight

A FEW MONTHS before undertaking the editing work of *Kaalam Mithya Aakkaatha Vaakku* (Words Undisputed by Time), a collection of critiques on Ayyappa Paniker's writings, Rajalakshmi S., Assistant Editor, State Institute of Encyclopaedic Publications, Thiruvananthapuram, asked me about the last poem Ayyappa Paniker had written. That took me back in time to the day when the news of his impending death was conveyed by his doctor.

The cause of Ayyappa Paniker's illness (and subsequent death) was interstitial lung disease. As his ailment became more serious, the oxygen-generating capacity of his lungs deteriorated considerably. One day, I took him to hospital for a scheduled medical examination. After his investigation, the doctor revealed to me that Ayyappa Paniker's chances of living beyond a month were remote. He said that he had given some indication regarding the condition to Ayyappa Paniker too. Usually, after every hospital visit, I stayed back with Ayyappa Paniker in his house and conversed with him for some time before going home. That day too, as we sat down to talk, he recited a few lines from Kadammanitta's *"Shanta"*, a work that has perhaps simultaneously troubled and mesmerised me more than any other poem:

> No more for us, a twilight.
> Though only a half-night is left,
> let us the remaining magical moments
> fill and enrich with meaning.

I told him that we should think of the work that needed to be done in the days that remained. He replied, "I have already written a poem about it." Regretting that I had not read it, I asked him which poem it was. "I wrote it only last night. The title is *Vella Meghangal* ("White Clouds")."

When I told Rajalakshmi that Ayyappa Paniker's last poem was "White Clouds", her reply conveyed a deep sense of gratification. Her guess or her conclusion had been right after all! She had placed that work at the very end of the trajectory of poetic journey that Ayyappa Paniker had undertaken. And how accurate she was! Where else was it possible to see the pure beauty of whiteness than in the clouds that wander aimlessly across the sky? That kind of reading which charted the course of Ayyappa Paniker's poetry prompted me to undertake another reading of his *Pathumanippookkal* (Poetry at Midnight).

The anthology contains short poems. There are very few compositions that extend beyond a page. The poems flowered out of the maturity that age and experiences had bestowed on Ayyappa Paniker. They are like conversational pieces, characterised by a complete avoidance of satire, black humour, irony, double entendres, suggestions, figures of speech and metre. Ayyappa Paniker's trademark irony and humour are conspicuous in their absence. They appear to be lines from his conversations with a friend or pieces of soliloquy. In fact, the last poem is titled "*Sambhashanam*" ("The Conversation"), and it contains a line that reads "Good poetry is conversation".

What we see in *Poetry at Midnight* is either a dip or a rise from the poems written until then (that is, the year 2000). Social criticism had always been a distinguishing mark of his poetry. The provocative curiosity of the earlier phase now gives way to sayings that inspire contemplation and reflection. The poems he composed after 2000, that is, after he crossed the age of 70, exude a fragrance of spiritual love that we associate with saints. The lines seem to have been forged in the smithy of a householder-ascetic's life experiences.

> These poems find the rainbow of human existence in the lives of the marginalised. Like drawing out a sacred river from a muddy pool using the power of meditation, the poet decants beauty even out of hunger and disease. The philosophy of love contained in these poems—that life is not about you and me; it contains all of us and others as well—raise them to the virtues of humans.

These lines, that form the blurb of the anthology, present the summary of its contents. The simple poetic lines from the pen of a poet who was considered the Master of Modernism, which during its heyday was considered inscrutable, are entirely different from the trends that had characterised his creative output until then. Perhaps that is why *Poetry at Midnight* has not attracted much critical attention. A few readers might even have said that such simple pieces were called poems only by virtue of the fact that they were written by Ayyappa Paniker. In these poems, Ayyappa Paniker uses the lingo of everyday life instead of serious literary language. Sometimes, they are like the lines we normally use while talking to very innocent kids:

> You may be from the south.
> I am a woman from the north.
> But when we come together
> This south and north will disappear.
> So let us start walking.
> You may hold my hand ("South and North", trans. P. Ravindran Nayar, *Poetry at Midnight*, Folio, 2010: 58).

In one of his YouTube speeches, Professor M. N. Karassery explains with the help of examples that friendship is the biggest wealth in the world. In *Poetry at Midnight*, Ayyappa Paniker uses the word "friend" no less than 62 times.

> Friend, I need
> Your blessing, your presence,
> Now more than ever before ("The Island", trans. P. Ravindran Nayar, *Poetry at Midnight*, Folio, 2010: 60).

The themes of love and friendship feature hugely in most of the poems. Love is beautiful because it comes from the heart—but friendship is extraordinarily beautiful since it encompasses a concern for another heart.

The themes of life and death do not enter the reader through bombastic words. Nor are they conveyed in heavy tones. There is a kind of pious indifference shown to both life and death. To those who view life ardently, the poems say that one has to discover meaning in the meaninglessness of life. The poet argues that there is no polarity in "South and North".

A few poems have the shadow of death cast on them. Yet he says:

> It is not the hardened minds, friend,
> But tender minds
> That deserve to be hailed Long Live.
>
> So, distressing experiences,
> Do keep my mind as a light breeze ("Light Breeze", trans. P. Ravindran Nayar, *Poetry at Midnight*, Folio, 2010: 28).

Poetry at Midnight constitutes the gospel of Ayyappa Paniker. The poems it contains are the thoughts that flowered in his mind; they are his sayings, his verse, his simple speeches. All the 62 poems were written in the initial years of the 21st century.

It may not be wrong to describe *Poetry at Midnight* as a compilation of his evening songs. They contain a rhythm that is not very pronounced. Rather, it is subtle. The poems picturise the spiritual beauty of everyday life, using the language of the common folk. They also present the formulas that he himself lived by.

In "*Palanirapacha*" ("Multicoloured Green"), the poet sees everything—compassion, humour, wrath and courage—as reflecting the various hues of green.

> A tinge of green
> Even in the greenish laughter of the green man
> From the green estuary, who is wont
> To masticate the green water ("Multicoloured Green", trans. P. Ravindran Nayar, *Poetry at Midnight*, Folio, 2010: 65).

In the last lines of the poem, the poet reveals his vision of life:

> I directly enquired.
> Friend said – in reality all are different colours
> And only he felt they were all green ("Multicoloured Green", trans. P. Ravindran Nayar, *Poetry at Midnight*, Folio, 2010: 65).

Ayyappa Paniker believed that humans had as much freedom as, or even more freedom than nature. For that reason, he attached a lot of importance to our choices and our decisions. But it appears that he was equally prepared to enjoy whatever life doled out to him. In the poem "The Peacock and the Moonlight", he wrote:

> It is not love
>
> Or tenderness alone
>
> That is sweet.
> There is sweetness
> Even in pain
> And the pang of separation (trans. P. Ravindran Nayar, *Poetry at Midnight*, Folio, 2010: 76).

By the time he comes to "The Wheel", he has accurately identified:

> You and I, friend, live
> In this rotation.
> All that happens is the rotation
> Of the wheel.
> It is not something
> Decided by you or me.
> Born somewhere,
> Growing up somewhere,
> You and I are destined
> To fall down somewhere.
> In between
> A slight drizzle,
> The touch of a peacock feather,
> Shadow of a rainbow,
> A slice of moonlight,
> A play of the eyes.
> Over. The wheel stops rotating.

So, friend,
Consider this as our auspicious moment.
Don't waste it.
Don't share it with anyone.
Mind and body will not always be
Soft and fleshy.

Look, even as we say this, that meteor
Has hurtled down, foamed and burnt out.
We too are like that ("The Wheel", ["Multicoloured Green"], trans. P. Ravindran Nayar, *Poetry at Midnight*, Folio, 2010: 54–55).

38
Variety and Contradictions

A FEW CRITICS have opined that many personalities resided within Ayyappa Paniker. If, like Fernando Pessoa, the literary genius of Portugal, Ayyappa Paniker had written under many pseudonyms, he might not have been recognisable as the author of all he wrote. "What is heard from one person/Are the soliloquies of many"—so he wrote in the poem "The Conversation" (trans. P. Ravindran Nayar, *Poetry at Midnight*, Folio, 2010: 93).

Elsewhere, he wrote:

> Nature loves variety. That is its nature and innate quality. Our readers need to understand that. I hope poets and critics too will (*Ayyappa Panikerude Lekhanangal 1980–90* [Ayyappa Paniker's Prose Writings, 1980–90], DC Books, 1990: 228).

In *Gotrayanam* ("Southbound"), he wrote, "when opposites meet, energy flows forever" (trans. Chitra Panicker, *Samyukta* VII, 1 [January 2007]: 169).

Ayyappa Paniker's poems are rich in opposites and contradictions. In the course of his speech delivered in 2022, Professor V.N. Murali, vice president of the Progressive Arts and Literature Society, said:

> Ayyappa Paniker's poems show a harmonious co-existence of contradictions. He brought a world of variety and contradictions into his poetry. Those poems discover that if there is big, there is small, and if there is darkness, there is light.

There are so many titles in his canon that celebrate opposites: "*Nee Njan*" ("You and I"), "*Sheriyum Thettum*" ("Right and Wrong"), "*Udayaasthamanam*" ("The Rising and Setting"], "*Pakalukal Ratrikal*" ("Days and Nights"), "*Thekkumvadakkum*" ("South and North"), "*Shatrumithram*" ("Enemy/Friend"), "*Gramanagaram*" ("Rural City"), "*Samhaarasrishti*" ("Destruction/Creation"), "*Puthanveetil Muthi*" ("The Old Woman in a New House") and many more! The very person who wrote "*Mrityupuja*" ("Hymn to Death") wrote "*Martyapuja*" ("Hymn to Man"). We do not have another poet in Malayalam who has celebrated opposites with so much gusto or studied them in as much depth as Ayyappa Paniker—curse and redemption, enemy-friend and fear of the enemy, rural city and urban village and so on. Not only did Ayyappa Paniker respect opposites, he also showed their confluence and complementarity in our lives, and this was the special feature of his poetry. He showed that it took the coming together of the positive and the negative to make light, to produce energy and to create life.

When Ayyappa Paniker walked with the members of his family along the canal close to his house in his native village, greeting his neighbours, exchanging pleasantries and sharing local jokes with them, with his *mundu* folded over his knees, he looked like a typical Kuttanad farmer. However, as he delivered a speech on the latest trends in avant-garde movements in world literature in universities across the world, he got transformed into an eminent critical genius. He was thus an amalgam of opposites.

In *Ayyappa Paniker: Jeevitharekha* (Ayyappa Paniker: Life Sketch), the poet C.S. Jayachandran observed that Ayyappa Paniker was a non-Romantic to the Romantics and a Romantic to the anti-Romantics (72). This contradiction is evident even within the ambit of a poem. "*Pakalukal Raatrikal*" ("Days and Nights") is a perfect example of such a phenomenon. Similarly, that the ultramodern poet who discarded metre completely in order to write his "*Nendravazhakolapatham*" ("Murder of a Banana Bunch") also wrote *Gopikadandakam*[1] ("The Song of the Cowherdess") has been praised as an unbelievable achievement. That the same poet also wrote "*Indan Ammavan*" ("Uncle Indan") and "*English Medium Pashu*" ("The English-Medium Cow") is another ironical fact. If most people find it difficult to conclude whether he was a scholar or a creative genius, it is because he occupied both extremes.

---

1 It is cast in the traditional Malayalam metre.

It is not possible to accurately pigeonhole Ayyappa Paniker because even while he was a part of everything, he was part of nothing. Was this because he always aligned himself with what was right? Or, was it because he was an opportunist? If we ask who opportunists are, we can define them as self-seeking individuals who indulge in activities that are totally opposed to what they have believed in and talked about over a long period of time. But Ayyappa Paniker's words and deeds were one and the same. Not only language and literature but the progress of other individuals too ranked very high in his list of priorities. However, when rightness changed according to persons, movements and situations, Ayyappa Paniker aligned himself with those changing configurations of rightness. Maybe that was why Satchidanandan, the poet, observed that Ayyappa Paniker's stance lay in his lack of one. He was subservient to none, and he reserved the prerogative to speak and act according to what he believed to be right in a given situation.

As he gave great importance to individual freedom in his life, he considered respecting others also very important. He did not permit any interaction to be a reason for others to fix a label on him. That was because he did not shy away from cooperating with people, no matter what religion they belonged to or what party they were members of, if it served a good cause. He did not emit to the outside world any clear-cut signals as to where his allegiance lay. To those who were always overzealous about affixing labels, he seemed to believe in what Soren Kierkegaard said, "Once you label me, you negate me."

True, he did not like being labelled, slotted or pigeonholed. Everyone is bound to experience shifts in tastes and affiliations. Mental attitudes are also likely to change. Stances too may alter. That is the fact of the human condition, but most of the time, we regard ourselves as intellectual beings, and for that reason make strident calls for constancy and argue for steadfastness. As long as there is no change, our assessment will be invariably correct – if an entity, regarding whom we have made an assessment, changes, we no longer feel confident about making any further evaluation. Ayyappa Paniker might have believed that since every single individual is likely to have multiple dimensions, we can understand life comprehensively only by accepting that multidimensionality along with all the thoughts and attitudes of different personalities at various points of time. And this is where we see virtue in Ayyappa Paniker's ability to perceive human beings as his raw material.

B. Sreekumar, in his book titled *Ayyappa Paniker: Cholkkazhachayum Chollaakkazhachayum*, records that while Ayyappa Paniker was a school-going child at Kavalam, he used to deliver letters to T.V. Thomas, the communist leader, who was then in hiding. As a student at Malabar Christian College in Kozhikode, Ayyappa Paniker had brief contacts with C. Achutha Menon and C. Unniraja that he has mentioned himself. In those days, weeklies like the *Deshabhimani* and *Janayugam* published his poems. He wrote poems about Che Guevara and Nicolas Guillen. Two of his closest literary friends—M.K. Sanoo and Kadammanitta Ramakrishnan— were MLAs who belonged to the communist front.

Another significant aspect of Ayyappa Paniker's personality was highlighted by Professor Murali in the course of his speech delivered in 2020 at the Dr Ayyappa Paniker memorial function organised by the Gandhinagar Residents' association, Vazhuthakkad, Thiruvananthapuram:

> It is doubtful whether we have adequately understood either Ayyappa Paniker or his literary works. Only if we recognise the importance of his native village of Kavalam can we fully appreciate Ayyappa Paniker. What he witnessed was a Kuttanad that was tearing down the foundations of feudalism. In that sense, he shared many similarities with Thakazhi Sivasankara Pillai (the novelist and short story writer). Both of them perceived and understood the steady growth of the organised strength of workers. They saw at close quarters how progressive ideas spread across the land and influenced the people tremendously.

Vinod Vaishakhi, the poet, observed in his article in *Kerala Kavitha*, 2007:

> A non-politician poet, who criticises the changes in politics from the outside, will be able to point out the failure of ideas and ask questions regarding it. For that very reason, Dr K. Ayyappa Paniker could become a constant presence in the unhindered flow of poetry (357).

A question which is difficult to answer is: Was Ayyappa Paniker a materialist or an ascetic? I have often felt that he lived like an ascetic in the midst of a materialistic world.

It is far more difficult to stay in the heart of a city, be involved in everything happening around you, and yet remain detached than to reside like a hermit in a forest far from the temptations and provocations of the world. Only an individual who has developed a plan that suits his or her vision, and lives according to it can manage to succeed.

Ayyappa Paniker did not attribute value to anything that this world, this materialistic world, cherished. Dr P.K. Rajan, the founder-editor of the *Littcrit* journal and former vice chancellor of Kannur University, said:

> His psychological stance is a unique one which is at once affiliated with and indifferent to all philosophies and schools of thought. He also gives the impression of being everywhere and yet being nowhere (*Ayyappa Paniker: Vyakthiyum Kaviyum* [Ayyappa Paniker: The Individual and the Poet], DC Books, 1990: 17).

In his introduction to the book *Kaalam Mithyayaakkaatha Vaakku* (Words Undisputed by Time), Dr P.P. Raveendran, the critic, wrote:

> In the final analysis, there is more logic in stating that what made Ayyappa Paniker a distinctive poet and thinker was not his modernism or postmodernism but rather his own life vision. In the absence of a specific word to describe this life vision or this ideology, let us call it critical humanism. Ayyappa Paniker's open mind, democratic awareness, critical intelligence, parodic skill, tolerant attitude towards opposing opinions and willingness to accept new ideas are all manifestations of his critical humanism (16).

39
Self-Masquerades

ONE DAY, WHEN I sought an appointment with Ayyappa Paniker, he said I could meet him at 4 in the evening. In reply, I informed him that Jessy would be accompanying me and he expressed happiness about it. We reached "Sarovaram", his house, on time. He seated us in his living room, and, after exchanging pleasantries with us for about five minutes, looked towards the inner room, and asked his daughter, "Meena, shouldn't we serve them tea?"

"Coming," she replied.

In a few minutes, Meena appeared, carrying a tray laden with teacups and plates of snacks. We told him the reason for the visit, had tea and snacks, and left "Sarovaram", contented.

In fact, we later realised that, having been informed beforehand, Ayyappa Paniker had prepared the tea himself and stored it in a flask. During the conversation, he asked his daughter for tea, and, without much delay, the tea was served. Few guests would imagine that Ayyappa Paniker himself brewed the tea and poured it into the flask minutes before their arrival. As they stepped into his house, Ayyappa Paniker welcomed them with a warm smile, extended hospitality and conversed with everyone.

Was this one of the several roles he played on the stage of life? Or, was it that he felt these were the ways to endure life? Was he putting into practice some of the philosophical insights he had gathered himself, customizing them as the occasions warranted? Was he simultaneously permitting life to move in its own manner, surviving its ebbs and its flows, and keeping it under control?

Can anyone who has seen Ayyappa Paniker, even if it was only once in their lifetime, recall his face that did not wear a smile or when he did not laugh? It is true that he was always seen as cheerful throughout his life. Everyone who recollects his expression will certainly remember the smile or the laugh that lit it all the time.

What was the meaning of it all? Was his life an exclusively happy one? Or, did he wear a smiling mask in front of others? Was it his conscious act of defence against the pains, sorrows and uneasiness that life had thrown in his path? Was the ever-smiling face a deliberately cultivated façade? Or, was it an inborn trait? The smile on his face faded only in the last days of his life when his body was wracked by pain, but even on those occasions, his words excited others to laughter.

This does not mean that Ayyappa Paniker never lost his temper, never showed irritation towards members of his family and his close associates or talk back to anyone. But it is not my intention to investigate whether he ever deviated from the personal code of conduct he had adhered to throughout his life.

Ayyappa Paniker showed us how life is all about giving oneself an intellectual training and finding a practical way of scooping out joy and satisfaction from the churn of sorrows, difficulties and crises. Although he wrote in "Epitaph" that life is about "patiently learning how not to live at all" (*Selected Poems of Ayyappa Paniker*, Modern Book Centre, 1985: 56), one has to assume that he thought about how to live, found the best way to do it, and followed the method he had arrived at.

Why did Ayyappa Paniker wear a hat? Was it symbolic? To some people who made enquiries, his repartee was "*Thottuthoppiyittatha...*"[1] To others, he said it was because he had a head! Although the two responses may be seen as a folk and an urban repartee respectively, they do contain a grain of truth.

In the poem "*Vaayana*" ("Reading"), he wrote:

> I cut off my head
> And bought a hat.

---

1 An idiom in Malayalam to indicate the state of abject defeat. It is popularly believed to have come from a historical event. When Tipu Sultan, the Tiger of Mysore (1751–99), invaded Malabar, he faced tough resistance. But he succeeded in vanquishing his opponents, and the defeated were forcibly converted to Islam and made to wear skullcaps.

Like poetry, goodness and humour, was self-masquerading too an inherent trait in Ayyappa Paniker? It was this quality in him that actually triggered my exploration into Ayyappa Paniker, the man. Two lines from the poem "*Aasakti*" ("Desire") are relevant in this context:

> That I conceal something
>
> is your anxiety, your suspicion.

Ayyappa Paniker is known primarily as a poet. Poetry-writing to him was an organic activity. Poets love and revel in the art of suggestion—not only what is explicitly stated but what is merely hinted at also has profound meaning in poetry. The world-famous poet Robert Frost was of the opinion that "Poetry provides the one permissible way of saying one thing and meaning another."

Ayyappa Paniker abandoned Romanticism that sought to exaggerate the mundane, and adopted modernism, which believed in uttering the truth in stark terms. But in doing so, he employed the techniques of humour, black humour, satire, oxymorons and ironical praise.

In his conversations, he invariably left his sentences incomplete. As a teacher too, it was not his practice to explain everything in great detail. He often left some space for students to think, investigate and discover things for themselves. But in his prose writings, he did not leave out anything. Even the humour in his prose passages was transparent and simple. His vocabulary in speeches and literary debates was simple and easy to understand.

In a sense, it could be argued that not only in the literary sphere but in his daily life too, Ayyappa Paniker was a poet. He preferred vagueness, which contained the possibility of multiple meanings, to clarity that conveyed only one meaning. In fact, he gave more importance to what was left unsaid than what was stated. In poetry, he could use irony to effect a complete concealment of meaning. But in real life what we confronted was an Ayyappa Paniker who indulged in interesting conversations, behaved in a heart-warming manner and wore a smile on his face.

He concealed both love and sorrow. There was a reason behind hiding affection. If anyone felt obliged, they were likely to display subservience in their behaviour and thoughts. What Ayyappa Paniker preferred, however, was equality. He might not have wanted anyone to show him respect. The reason for concealing sorrow was that he did not look for anyone's pity. What Changampuzha and Sanjayan (the pseudonym of Manikoth Ramunni Nair, a writer in Malayalam) have said is relevant in this context. Although a sense of humour was an inborn talent, it might have served to keep his sorrow under wraps.

Rene Descartes who said, "He who hid well, lived well," found inspiration in Ovid's *"Bene qui latuit bene vixit"* (found in *Tristia*, composed by Ovid during his exile) which means to live well is to live unnoticed. It is about living a quiet life of obscurity, unencumbered by the disappointments that may come with conspicuity. He who does not seek fame, lives well.

Ayyappa Paniker never became well-known as a spiritual guru or social reformer like Gandhiji, Sree Narayana Guru or Chattambi Swami. Nor is he considered so. Gandhiji, Sree Narayana Guru and Chattambi Swami considered it their bounden duty to cleanse human beings, and make them love their fellow-creatures. I do not know if Ayyappa Paniker felt that to be his, but as we observe him from close range, we cannot rule out that possibility. He took secret pride in being a humanistic *karma yogi*. It may not be wrong to even claim that he tried to conceal that fact from the eyes of the world. We can reach such a conclusion only through the hints he dropped, his actions, his humour, the virtues of others that he sought to highlight, and so on. Perhaps he was conscious of the fact that doing moral propaganda work was not his forte. There are no indications which suggest that even as he lived, he wished to be known as a virtuous or saintly person (we are not sure whether he thought along those lines at all!). Ayyappa Paniker had the talent to bring out the best in us but made us feel that we discovered it ourselves. Sadly, however, this aspect of his personality is not subjected to analysis. Critical focus is almost exclusively on his literary personality.

Sree Narayana Guru taught us how to lead a good life. He led by example and conveyed his thoughts through his poetic writings as well. But he is known as a spiritual leader and social reformer rather than as a poet. Ayyappa Paniker created the impression that he was involved only in literary activities, but through his own life and his poems he showed us how to lead a good life without, however, uttering a single explicit word about it. That is the reason why he continues to be known and assessed only as a poet. Cherishing *sattvic* qualities in his mind, he practised them in his day-to-day activities to achieve a peaceful and harmonious attitude – although he lived like a *sanyasi*, his self-masquerades made it impossible for many to discover that he was one.

40
Writing the Self

D R THOMAS MATHEW, the critic who enjoyed a close friendship with Ayyappa Paniker, wrote that

> ... the sheer volume of work, that afforded no reprieve, as well as his sense of humour was what helped Paniker get relief from the burns caused by sorrows that were severe enough to send anyone to the edge of suicide or to a mental asylum (*Kerala Kavitha*, 2007: 263).

But we know that alongside heavy, endless work and humour, poetry too rescued him from such calamities:

> We first met at the promontory that
> Is thought to have hidden danger
> How did you reach there?
> You may say, like others, that
> Life brought you here.

All have learnt to say so.

I came not because of life,
But because of lack of it.
A lifelessness that denied me even sleep.
I came to this promontory out of sheer boredom.
When I saw you here I was perplexed.
Were you in such a plight as to come here?

This promontory had invited many
To it and blessed them.
But we did not get that blessing.
After our meeting then
This place was out of mind for quite some time.
Now we come here again.
For what purpose?
To see the view from this point?
Or to confirm its bad name? ("Danger", trans. P. Ravindran Nayar, *Poetry at Midnight*, Folio, 2010: 20).

In this poem, we witness a person escape danger.

When we examine such autobiographical pieces very closely, we notice many sad and stormy life situations that are characterised by lifelessness or meaninglessness. Ayyappa Paniker did not wear his heart on his sleeve and did not share his troubles or his sorrows with anyone. Perhaps some of the most poignantly poetic lines ever penned in Malayalam came from Ayyappa Paniker's pen.

One of his noteworthy poems, "*Mrityupuja*" ("Hymn to Death"), shook the consciousness of Malayalis, by its theme and its treatment. The poet Vishnu Narayanan Namboothiri remarked that he spent a troubled and sleepless night after reading the lines that were written as an invitation to death. Making no attempts to conceal his feelings, Vishnu Narayanan Namboothiri wrote, "That poem, which beckons all creatures to the pitch-black, new moon night of sleep, shrivelled me with its own dark power".

The lines that most overwhelmed him were:

> Come,
> slow-moving,
> black-complexioned
> winter night,
> come!
> ....
> No more of these,
> the morning rays:
> neither day nor daylight.
> Come down for ever,
> O winter night,
> dissolve the frozen nerves
> of this world! ("Hymn to Death", *Selected Poems of Ayyappa Paniker*, Modern Book Centre, 1985: 34–36).

This was written when Ayyappa Paniker was only 38 years old. What he wrote at 50 was darker still:

> Out of all these you have made for me this life, O Mother,
> Out of all these you have made for me this body too.
> But why haven't you, Mother, put any poison into it?

Why haven't you, Mother, given me the poison teeth?
("Poison", trans. K. Ayyappa Paniker, *Days and Nights*,
National Educational Research Centre, 2001: 220).

When the romantic lines of a very popular film song—
"Will You give me another birth on these beautiful, Heaven-
like shores . . ."[1]—filled the air, Ayyappa Paniker penned a
verse about the cruelties and pain bestowed by real life:

> Since you ask
> shouldn't I reply?
> Never again, ever,
> a rebirth for me.
> One itself, sufficient!
> Never again, ever
> death, birth and rebirth.
> A new house?
> A new mother?
> A new childhood?
> New challenges?
> New temptations?
> New bruises?
> New sense of rhythm?
> Ever new promises?
> Never again, ever. ("Never Again, Ever")

The next poem is written from the bog of misery. It was
published twice and bore different titles – "Self-Curse" and

---

[1] The famous lines of Vayalar Ramavarma (1928–75) which featured in the film *Kottaaram Vilkkaanundu* (1975).

"Without Waking Up". Only the first and last two lines are quoted below:

> Every day as I lie down to sleep,
> a drop wells up in the eye ...
> One day while sleeping, with tear-filled eyes,
> let me not wake up, ever.

Ayyappa Paniker's mother died just when he stepped into his teens. Thereafter, his elder sister took on a maternal role and raised her younger siblings, without giving them an opportunity to miss their mother. The tears that welled up in Ayyappa Paniker's eyes, whenever he remembered her, took the form of a poem titled "*Kannamma*":

> Like fresh dreams on teary eyes,
> dawns and nights, Kannamma counts.

All the love and respect he had for his elder sister is evident in "*Kaaliyoottu*":

> Not a day, nor a night passes
> Without getting soggy in your memory.

But by the end of "*Kaaliyoottu*", Kannamma's teardrops flow as drops of blood as her heart breaks:

> If unable I become to come in front of you
> like this, and sing my song, grown old,
> the blood that trickles from my broken heart,
> please accept – O Devi! – as an offering
> and bestow your kind blessing.

It is said that "*Thilahomam*" ("Ancestor Worship") was a poem that burst out of Ayyappa Paniker on the very day he came to learn that a loved one was in the grip of an incurable disease:

> Today I can't do anything.
> Thinking of you, I can't stop the throbs of weeping.
> Lying in the bitter darkness in my eyes
> to chant the dawn prayers,
> henceforth, I can't, I can't, Mother!
> Seeing the beginning as the end, O Rebirth!
> I can't remain without doing anything.
> Seeing the whole earth, ulcer-covered,
> no matter what it thinks about, the mind
> can't help getting burnt, can't but weep …

There are other poems which are his soliloquies in which Ayyappa Paniker plunges into the deep end of his own life. "*Minnaminungu*" ("The Fire-fly") for instance:

> I remember my friendless childhood,
> Lonely teens, the arrogance
> Of bouncing youth and
> The marital-widowhood that came subsequently.
>
> Come, fire-fly, come into my room.
> Sit on my bed. Wink your eyes again.
> Spread your broken light in this small room,
> In my mind as well (trans. P. Ravindran Nayar, *Poetry at Midnight*, Folio, 2010: 79).

As his wife was ill, Ayyappa Paniker had to take on kitchen responsibilities. He even wrote a few kitchen-poems like "*Ee Aanungalkenda Paatram Thechaalu*" ("Why Can't Men Wash Dishes?"). Only someone who has spent considerable time in the kitchen can truly understand life from a woman's perspective in Kerala. As his wife's illness worsened, his affection and concern for her deepened.

His actions may also have been one of the factors that, following his death, stirred the sense of humanism in his daughter Meena's husband Sunil, inspiring him to care for his mother-in-law as if she were his own mother, take her to the hospital whenever required, and look after her until her death. It is in this context that many have pointed to Ayyappa Paniker's personal life in his poem "*Kilimaram*" ("Hill Mango").

> If the hill mango does not bloom
> should we chop it?
> If the hibiscus does not fruit
> should we uproot and discard it?
> If the milk yield is low
> should we kill the cow?
> If raped, does my mother
> cease to be my mother?

"Upon My Walls" might be considered Ayyappa Paniker's first attempt at writing about the self. "*Kudumbapuranam*" ("The Family Saga"), "*Kuttanadan Drishyangal*" ("Kuttanad Sights"), "*Kavalam*" and other poems are about his family roots, native village and the paths he traversed. Poems like

"*Pakalukal Ratrikal*" ("Days and Nights") and "Passage to America" describe some of the intense experiences he had during his research period in the US.

Most people are of the opinion that *Gotrayanam* ("Southbound") was a poem Ayyappa Paniker consciously crafted to narrate the history of himself and his family in the form of a clan's journey. The poem hints that Ayyappa Paniker had arrived at a philosophy according to which we can continue living only if we sublimate our big sorrows and ignore the small ones:

> Shove away small griefs
> with your fingertip,
> only the great sorrows
> bury deep in the heart;
> for them to sleep soft,
> make your breast a cradle.
> If compassion and song
> Mix with enough humour,
> we can embark upon
> life's terrific trip (trans. Chitra Panicker, *Samyukta* VII, 1, January 2007: 169).

In "*Maranathinippuram*" ("On This Side of Death"), the poet presents a wasted life:

> In this strange
> morning hour,
> when the spread-out feather too
> withers and falls,
> the earth weeps.

But what the final lines point to is the possibility of survival:

> Those who crow over
> the morning light,
> those who condemn
> the dark night,
> those who remember
> philosophy of old legends,
> those who sound
> the clarion call of novelty,
> let them raise their arms
> and wave widely.
> Let them sing
> full-throatedly.

Just as there are a few poems that reflect the days of conflicts and sorrows that Ayyappa Paniker underwent, there are others that speak of survival and self-confidence like "*Martyapuja*" ("Hymn to Man"), "Hey, Gagarin!", "*Agnipuja*" ("Fire Worship"), "*Maranithinippuram*" ("On This Side of Death"), "*Pookkaathirikkaan Enikkavathille*" ("I Can't Help Blossoming") and "*Yauvanam*" ("Youth").

> Without you, will rise not the sun,
> Without you, will spin not the earth,
> Without you, will move not the world,
> Will glow not the moon, will heave not the sea,
> Will rise, dance, sway, spread or glow not
> The fire, without you.

> O human! Without you, without you
> Will not fly, will not sing, the bird ("*Martyapuja*"
> ["Hymn to Man"]).

In "*Yauvanam*" ("Youth"), we see Ayyappa Paniker ask the god of life for one more year of youth:

> For one more year
> Give me my youth.
>
> Who is the master of all life on earth?
> Let him bestow on me a new youthfulness.
>
> I am not content yet with the flowers and fruits
> That give sweetness to my zest and lust.
>
> If not for one year, for one year more
> Give me my sensual youth (trans. P. Ravindran Nayar, *Poetry at Midnight*, Folio, 2010: 81).

If hope glows robustly in some poems like "*Agnipuja*" ("Fire Worship") and "*Martyapuja*" ("Hymn to Man"), utter pessimism weighs down certain others like "*Mrityupuja*" ("Hymn to Death"). Baffled after reading the poems of Ayyappa Paniker that conveyed totally different mental attitudes and adopted even opposing stances towards life and death, Vishnu Narayanan Namboothiri wrote a letter to the poet with the query: "'*Agnipuja*' or '*Mrityupuja*' – which one of the two reflects your real face?" The reply that came promptly was: "Got your letter. A nice missive. I too am in search of the real face."

"*Sambhashanam*" ("The Conversation"), one of his last poems gives us an accurate picture:

> Can't you write a poem
> Whatever you speak of me?
> When the symbol itself becomes symbolic
> It will not be possible to assert this is that.
> Only we will understand, but
> Sometimes even we may not understand (trans. P. Ravindran Nayar, *Poetry at Midnight*, Folio, 2010: 93).

41
Conclusion

AS THE COMMON public and the intellectuals focused on Ayyappa Paniker's creativity, scholarship and cultural contributions, the gaze of all was directed only towards those aspects of his personality. Since he taught literature, teaching, delivering speeches on and propagating the value of goodness were not his preoccupations. That is perhaps the reason why we do not view or study him seriously as a social reformer or an eminent ascetic. I do not argue that those who have written about him have not mentioned anything about the values that governed his life (M.K. Sanoo's *Ayyappa Panikerum Ayyappa Panikerum* [Ayyappa Paniker and Ayyappa Paniker] certainly mentions them). But, generally speaking, attention has always been paid to his literary contributions alone.

If anyone were to ask me whether Ayyappa Paniker, who lived in this world from 1930 to 2006, should be recommended for a kind of secular beatification, I cannot claim to have an answer. Our society has readers who cherish noble desires in life. If this book serves to enthuse them or warm their hearts, I will feel gratified. There is a lot we can learn from this writer we love, in his avatars as a private individual and as a poet. (Much of which can be implemented in our own lives as well.) The reason is that he did not see his personal and poetic lives as two distinct entities. Maybe that is why he continues to remain a font of inspiration.

> You are not a stone.
> You should not become one.
> You are energy, you are the source,
> An ever-flowing river of song ("The Stone", trans. P. Ravindran Nayar, *Poetry at Midnight*, Folio, 2010: 89).

These days, spicy controversies are what make hits. It is doubtful whether there will be readers for stories about noble persons. The apprehensions that Ayyappa Paniker articulated about C. Unniraja, using the Kathakali metaphor, applies equally to him:

> Will history ignore mild-natured people?... Spectators will sit up and notice only when demonic characters come onstage and roar.... Whoever notices those who string idealistic dreams on lotus silk? (*Vyakthichitrangal Yaatradrishyangal* [Personal Profiles, Travel Sights], Cultural Publications Department, Government of Kerala, 2005: 98).

Ayyappa Paniker led life as a very ordinary person, like many of us. But he had the extraordinary ability to transform a worm into a butterfly. I feel gratified, that driven by curiosity, I could weave my way through the magical lines written by a genius who, exuding goodness, wrote:

> How very generous –
> the buds of flame of human love
> on the seven-wick lamp
> that glows every twilight! (Ayyappa Paniker, "*Kudumbapuraanam*" [The Family Saga]).

In the poem "*Puzhu*", he wrote:

> The worm asked:
> Are you a worm?
>
> I am not so fortunate.
> The condition is far worse now, sir.
> . . . .
> When you touched me
> I turned into a butterfly.
> Look, how beautiful my wings are!
> If I sit on a flower
> I will look like a flower.
> It was you who made me beautiful, friend ("The Worm", trans. P. Ravindran Nayar, *Poetry at Midnight*, Folio, 2010: 69–70).

Throughout his life, Ayyappa Paniker was absorbed in the task of converting the worm into a butterfly. He felt that ensuring the well-being and progress of his fellow humans was his responsibility too. And that was how he led his life as a *karma yogi* in the cultural field of Kerala. That is the reason why despite the passage of time, following his death, Ayyappa Paniker continues to inspire and influence a lot of people.

In his poem "Epitaph", he wrote:

> Here lies the body of Mister Panicker
> who at the end of his panicking days
> agreed to lie still for a while.
> It's not known what happened to his soul
> if indeed he ever had one.
> He wasn't quite unlike any of us while he lived:
> ....
> all his life he was patiently
> learning how not to live at all (*Selected Poems of Ayyappa Paniker*, Modern Book Centre, 1985: 56).

We are patiently learning how to live, taking a leaf out of his book.

In "*Aarundivide Charitrathodu Samvadikkan Ponnavar*" ("Who Here Is Capable of Conversing with History?"), he wrote:

> I am a human, I loved this world
> more than the world loved me.
> But did I love?
> I did not beg for love. That is not to beg for.
> That is to give. But did I give?

You did, sir. There are several of us who experienced and enjoyed your love, the memories of which infuse enthusiasm in us to this day.

Let me conclude by quoting the lines he wrote in *Vyaktichitrangal Yaatradrishyangal* ("Personal Profiles, Travel Sights"):

> When we swim towards memories of old times, we become young. As we emerge from it, we forget old age. On remembering that beyond a string of material and temporary losses, there are such fragrant loving moments in human life, many complaints about life are forgotten. Only that life is well-lived which allows memories of good things.

Index

Aadhunikothara Kavitha 18–19, 21, 23
Abraham, John, film director 20–23, 108–09
Achutha Menon, C. 160, 179–80, 206
Adhikarasaurabhyam 183, 192
Adhunika Kavithayude Jeerna Mukham xi, 56, 146, 150
Aesthetes xii, 57, 64–65, 86, 152
Agnipuja 5, 100, 224–25
Agraharathil Kazhuthai 20
Aksharam 14
Allegiance 57, 106, 178, 205
Ananthamurthy, Dr U.R. 25, 42, 142, 173
Anthology(ies) xi, xii, 13, 18, 30, 33, 89, 106, 115, 165, 174, 182, 186–87, 196–97
Appukuttan Nair 66, 141
    Margi 66, 141
Aravindan, Govindan 15–16, 22, 52, 140
Asan World Prize for poetry 182, 190
Atholi, Raghavan 44–45
Attitude xi, 31, 49, 61, 94, 131, 161, 169, 192, 206, 208, 215, 225
Ayyappa Paniker Forever 36, 83, 133

Ayyappa Paniker Foundation 152
Ayyappa Paniker: Jeevitharekha 52, 97, 188, 204
Ayyappa Paniker Memorial Lecture 173
Ayyappa Panikerude Kritikal xi
Ayyappa Panikerude Lekhanangal: 1950–80 100, 125, 149, 165
Ayyappa Panikerude Lekhanangal: 1980–90 149, 202
Ayyappa Panikerude Lekhanangal: 1990–2005 164
Ayyappa Panikerude Narmasambhashanangalum Narmakavithakalum 71
Ayyappa Paniker: Vyakthiyum Kaviyum 59, 62, 65–66, 155, 208

Balakrishnan, P.K. 55
Basheer, Dr M.M. 58, 118, 175
Basheer, Vaikom Muhammad 1, 4, 71
Basic Malayalam 112–13
Beckett, Samuel 2, 41, 90, 140
    Godoye Kaathu 41, 90, 140
Behaviour 8, 48, 61, 85, 94, 173, 192, 213
Bhashaposhini 60, 84, 95–97, 130, 137, 141
Booker Prize 127

Central Sahitya Akademi 92, 138
Chakram 41, 102
Cinema/film 14–15, 20–22, 29–30, 42, 47, 53, 57, 64, 66, –68, 107–08, 127–28, 138, 162, 219
Compassion xi, 133, 135, 199, 223
Conversation(s) xviii, 22, 24, 66, 71, 74, 98, 124–25, 141, 144, 147, 156, 158, 166, 173, 182, 186, 192, 196, 212, 21 – 3
Creativity xiii, 32, 175, 227
Criticism(s) 48, 56, 61, 83, 147, 149, 152, 196
Critic(s) 13, 15, 25–26, 42, 57, 60, 87, 92, 94, 115, 117, 130, 146–48, 172, 202, 208, 216
Culture 12, 17, 21, 60, 64, 66, 72, 91, 97, 113, 142, 152, 161, 169
  anarchic intellectual 21
  dramatic 66
  laissez-faire 12
  Western 169

Das, Kamala 6, 26, 186
Dathan, B.D. 66, 103–04
  Ayyappa Paniker: Jeevitharekha 104, 204
Deivathar 68
Democracy 105, 183
Democrat, The 61
  "T. S. Eliot" 61
Department of Malayalam, University of Kerala 115
Deshamangalam 181
Devan, M.V. 26, 66, 105–06
Dhanya 35–36
Differences of opinion 60, 160
Drama 43, 47, 53, 64–65, 73

Eliot, T.S. 61, 100, 165, 181
  Waste Land, The 85, 100, 103, 181
Emergency of 1975 4–5, 77, 128, 160, 179

Emotions xix, 53, 65, 149, 162, 165
Encouragement 90, 92, 95, 105, 141–42
Ente Bhithimel xi, 101, 165–66, 222
Epitaph xiii, 93, 165, 211, 230
Expression ix, xii, 158, 177, 191, 210

Fiction 47
Freedom 4, 10, 34, 58, 91, 116, 125, 128, 158, 181, 199, 205
  individual 4, 181, 205
Friendship 10, 21, 34, 44, 60, 89, 94, 96, 139–40, 154, 170, 175, 192, 197–98, 216

Gandhi, Mahatma 36, 38, 45, 128, 149, 165, 214
Generosity xiii, 18, 45, 84, 139
Gopikadandakam 76, 157, 204
Gotrayanam 105, 107, 135, 203, 223
Gramanagaram 203
Gratitude 37, 132, 138, 152, 169–70, 185
Guild Soft, software company 45, 120, 122
Guru 10, 50, 94, 104, 118, 122, 139, 150, 158, 164, 171–72, 185, 214
  status of a 118
Gurukulam system of education 10
Guru-shishya bond 94, 122

Haasan, Kamal 138
  Sakshibhootham 138
Harris, Dr V.S. 36–37
Himalayan 79
Homer 128–29
  Iliad 128–29

Index

Humanism 46, 91, 100–101, 161, 182, 208, 222
Humility 8, 124, 155, 157, 180, 193
Humour 11, 24, 34, 61, 68, 71–72, 74–75, 77, 79, 81–83, 85, 104, 110, 124, 137, 147, 158, 196, 199, 212–14, 216, 223
  black 34, 77, 124, 158, 196, 212

Illustrations 41, 95, 105, 107
Indan Ammavan 204
Indian Administrative Service (IAS) 139, 157
Indiana University, US 8, 58, 176
Innale Njaan Whitmane Kandu 8
Inspiration 7, 66, 213, 228
Institute of English, University of Kerala xvii, 5, 7, 10–11, 13, 17, 28, 34, 44, 48, 60, 129, 133–34, 139, 185, 192

Jacob, Lizzie 66, 104–05, 139
Jayachandran, C.S. 97, 117, 204
  Ayyappa Paniker: Jeevitharekha 104, 204
Jessy, wife xv, 88, 128, 131–32, 209
Jojo, B.C. 108–09, 121–22, 140, 144
Joke(s) 9, 26, 34, 68, 71–72, 74, 77, 84, 96, 110, 112, 121, 170, 192, 204
Journalism 15, 34, 40, 48, 127
  aggressive style of 48
Joyce, James 128, 129
  Portrait of the Artist as a Young Man, A 128–29

Kabir Samman 189
Kadukka 5, 178
Kareem, Dr N.A. 153–54
Karma yogi 161, 214, 230
Karnad, Girish 54–55
Kavalam 65, 73, 222

Kavithalaya 186
Kaviyarangu 30, 41–42
Kavya Bharati 186
Kerala
  College campuses in 30, 178
  cultural landscape of 3
  cultural sphere in 27
  foundation for science and technology in 120
  literary community 15
  Malayalam dailies in 152
  politicisation of 179
Kerala Bhasha Institute 16, 31, 104
  B.D. Dathante Vaakkum Varayum 104
Kerala Kavitha x, 13, 28, 33, 44–45, 53, 58, 84, 89, 91, 94–95, 105, 118–19, 139–40, 143, 157, 171, 207, 216
Kerala Sahitya Akademi 33, 41, 192
Kerala Sahitya Akademi Award 33, 41
Kerala University Union 75, 142
Krishna Kumar (Atmaraman) 60, 129, 130, 143, 169
Krishna Kumar, K. 37, 143, 169
Krishnan Nair, M. 15
  Sahitya Vaaraphalam 15
Krishna Pillai, Changampuzha 79, 149, 189
Krishna Warrier, N.V. 90, 146, 149
Kudumbapuranam 5, 125, 222, 229
Kunhiraman, Kanayi 66, 105, 142
Kurukshetram xii, 5, 100–101, 103
Kurup, O.N.V. 57–58, 112, 181
Kuttanadan Drishyangal 222

Language and literature xvii, 1, 4–5, 7–8, 12, 14–17, 21, 30, 47, 54, 67, 73, 82, 85, 88, 91, 94–95, 105–06, 112–13, 127, 129, 137,

142–44, 147–48, 152–53, 160, 162, 171, 174–75, 185, 187, 189, 197, 199, 204–05, 227
  American 8
  contemporary 175
  English xvii, 1, 3, 5–7, 10–11, 13, 17, 28, 34, 36, 42, 44, 48, 54, 57, 60, 73, 82, 85, 91, 93, 113, 121, 129, 133–34, 138–39, 143, 153, 157, 169, 174–75, 185–86, 192, 204
  Hindi 114, 142
  Kannada 54, 142, 181
  Malayalam xvii, 1, 4–8, 12, 15–16, 29–30, 43, 45, 54–57, 59, 66, 69, 71–73, 77, 84, 87–88, 90, 93, 96–97, 107, 112–13, 115, 118, 121–23, 137–38, 140, 143, 146, 152–53, 157, 165–66, 171, 174–75, 181, 189–90, 203–04, 211, 213, 217
  Marathi 142
  mild 82, 147, 160
  modernist 15
  refined 152
  regressive tendencies in 47
  Tamil 73, 138, 142
Lanka Lakshmi 53, 72, 141
Lankesh, Palya 25, 39, 142
Lankesh Patrike 39
Literary
  critic 15, 94
  discussions 14, 174
  sensibility 12, 18
  works xvii, 1, 29, 161, 207
Littcrit 186, 208
Loka Malayali 110

Madhavikutty (Kamala Surayya/Das) 1, 6, 26
Madhu, Kilimanoor, film actor 107, 109, 117, 141

Mahatma Gandhi (MG) University, Kottayam 36, 45, 142
Malayala Cinema 42
Malayala Manorama 84, 108–09, 152
Malayalis 65, 77, 90, 108, 112–13, 178, 217
Mangalath, Priyadas G. ix–x, xiii–v, xix, 17, 44, 109, 132
  academic career 34, 40, 42
  founder-editor of *Sankramanam* 12
  Master's course in journalism 13, 34
  Paniker sir, my poet-father 45
  stress and sadness congeal on my face 26
Martyapuja 5, 100, 203, 224–25
Marx, Karl 82
  Das Kapital 82
Mathew, Dr M. Thomas 3, 147, 216
Media xviii–ix, 12, 16, 143
Meena, Ayyappa Paniker's daughter 61, 209, 222
Minnaminungu 221
Modernism 2–3, 12–13, 16–17, 20, 47–49, 85, 152, 197, 208, 212
Mrityudarshanam 124
Mrityupuja x, 5, 30, 32, 147, 203, 217–18, 225
Mukundan, Maniyambath 1, 32, 52
  Anchara Vayassulla Kutty 32
Music 21, 57, 105, 147

Namboothiri, Vishnu Narayanan 85–86, 90, 218, 225
Nangyarkoothu 66
Narayanan, K.C. 151–52
  Nammude Kavikal Ee Mattil Aavathirikkatte 151
National Educational Research

Centre (NERC) 63, 77, 100, 219
Days and Nights 77, 100
Navadhara Publishing Cooperative Society xi, 32
Naveena Natakam 42
Nee Njan 203
Nendravazhakolapatham 204
Nishkama karma 161, 169
Niyogam 13, 122
Njan Oru Tyagi 78
Nobel Prize for Literature 90, 175, 181
Novels 1, 30, 41, 44, 46, 122, 127–28, 138, 142–43

Padmanabhan, Neela 69, 138, 142–43
Painting and sculpture 103, 105–06, 142
Pakalukal Ratrikal 3, 5, 30, 63, 77, 100, 178, 203–04, 219, 223
Panachippuram, Jose 84, 139–40
Panangad, Pradeep 16
  Malayala Samanthara Masika Charitram 16
Panicker, Chitra 136, 203, 223
  Samyukta VII 203, 223
Panicker, Kavalam Narayana 64–65, 117
  Sopanam 65
Panicker, Narayana 64–65, 117
Panicker, Renji 14, 56
  Ee Jeernicha Mukham Adhunika Kavithayudeyo Marxian Nirupanathinteyo 56
Paniker, Dr K. Ayyappa
  90th birth anniversary celebrations 68, 187
  a committed teacher 174
  a cultural sanyasi 156
  a guide and source of support 156
  a great Malayalam poet 123
  a true Gandhian 165
  a visiting professor in more than 20 foreign universities 175
  as a powerhouse of ideas 144
  as a social reformer 214
  as a spiritual guru 214
  as an adviser 186
  as guru 10, 139
  as the Master of Modernism 152
  cause of illness 194
  classes on Whitman 9
  conversations or speeches xviii, 74, 98, 147, 156, 192, 196, 212
  creativity and goodness xiii, 227
  critics of 147
  death of 145, 154
  doctoral degree from Indiana University 58, 176
  encouragement 90
  extraordinariness of x
  facial expression ix, 177
  feature of humanistic creative work 95
  foreword to Tatvamasi 81
  friends 105, 142, 206
  friendships 96, 175
  generosity xiii, 45
  greatness of 187
  humaneness xii
  humans as his medium 142–43
  humility 124
  humour 24, 71, 74, 82, 110
  image of the most recognised poet-translator-scholar in Malayalam 7
  influence of 97
  intellectual intervention of 129
  intellectual support 186
  jokes 9, 68, 110
  last poem 194–96
  leadership 65, 118

lifestyle 38
love for poetry and literature 30
loyalty 169
made reader of English at the Institute 153
noble intent 115
Passage to America 8, 223
patronage of 12
personality x, xiii, 88, 97, 142, 153, 155, 157, 173, 193, 207, 214, 227
personal life 164, 222
philosophy 111
poem/poetry x, xvii–iii, 5, 9, 16, 33, 52, 56, 59–60, 62, 79, 90, 99, 110, 116, 118–19, 121, 138, 142, 149, 158, 187, 195–96, 203, 206, 214
policy 116
principle of life 46
private conversations 166
quality of nature x
recommendations 122
responses 46, 54, 74
serious approach towards research scholars 9
speeches and articles 93
spiritual guidance of 65
spoke about the Lankesh model 40
style of 9, 116, 149, 156
support 42, 43, 66
the Master of Modernism 152, 197
thoughts 182
tribute to 36
vision of life 199
works 32, 152
writings 194
Panineerpoovu 166
Pathumanippookkal 53, 100, 169, 195

Phalithan 77
Pillai, Muraleedharan (Murali) 65, 72, 141, 207
Pinnem Chankaran xi, 146, 150
Playwrights 53, 65–66, 181
Poems/Poetry
　appreciation of 117, 169
　cartoon 76–77, 105
　eponymous 106
　humourous 77
　kitchen- 222
　Malayalam 6–7, 77, 88, 96, 118, 171, 181, 189
　modernist xi, 2, 30, 56, 58, 146, 150
　reading sessions 13, 96, 115
Poet-friends 65, 171
Poetic performances 52, 65
Poetry-writing x, 93, 149, 151, 166, 185–86, 212
Poets' meetings/meets ix, xiv, xvii, 27, 28, 75–76, 85, 175
Politics 4, 64, 160, 178, 182–83, 207
Pookkathirikkan Enikkaavathille 70, 106, 224
Postmodernism 17, 118, 208
Power 50, 67, 80, 88, 139, 157, 161, 183, 188–89, 192, 196, 218
　dark 218
　Inspirational 139
Prasad, Narendra 3, 16, 24, 51, 64–65
　Natya Griham 65
Prathikoolikalum (mattu koolikalum) 85
Progressive Arts and Literature Society 203
Prose writings 71, 147, 212
Puthanveetil Muthi 203
Puzhu 229

Raghavan Pillai, Edappally 189
Rajan, Dr P.K. 37, 186, 208
Rajasekharan, P.K. 13, 172
Rajeevan, T.P. 97, 117, 137
Ramakrishna Panikkar,
    M.R.(Kadammanitta) 2–3, 20,
    22, 24, 30, 71, 90–91, 95, 140,
    181, 195, 206
Ramakrishnan, Deshamangalam
    45, 93–94, 114–15, 117
Ramakrishnan, Kadammanitta 90,
    140, 206
    Devisthavam 30
    Kaattaalan 30
    Kattaalan 90
    Kozhi 90
    Kurathi 30, 90
    Shanta 3, 90, 195
Ramakrishnan, Malayattoor 41
    Verukal 41
    Yakshi 41
    Yanthram 41
Ramanujan, A.K. 142, 161
    *Kaalam Mithyayaakkaatha
        Vaakku* 208
Ravindran Nayar, P. 53–54, 102,
    140, 169, 197–202, 217, 221,
    225–26, 228–29
    Poetry at Midnight (trans.) 53,
        100, 102, 194–202, 217, 221,
        225–26, 228–29
Recitals and performances 3, 30,
    65, 90
Recitations 3–4, 86
Religion 100, 191, 205
Rushdie, Salman 127–28
    Midnight's Children 127–28
    Satanic Verses, The 127–28

Sahitya Akademi function,
    Ernakulam 54
Sambhashanam 196, 202, 226

Samyukta 136, 185
Sankaran, Thayat xi, 56, 146, 150
    *Adhunika Kavithayude Jeernicha
        Mukham* xi, 56, 146
Sankara Pillai, K.G. (K.G.S.) 65,
    95–96, 117, 173, 181, 187
    Nataka Kalari 65
Sankramana Kavitha Vedi 114,
    115, 116, 117, 118, 119
    first meeting of 114
Sankramanam x, xvii, 12–19,
    21–22, 25, 28, 30–31, 39–42,
    47–52, 56, 66, 94, 112, 135, 171,
    176, 178
Sankramanam Pustaka Chakram 41
Sankramana Sandhya 13, 25
Sanoo, M.K. xv, 16, 26, 49, 87–88,
    192, 206, 227
    *Ayyappa Paniker: Nishedhathinte
        Charu Roopam* 88
    *Ayyappa Panikerum Ayyappa
        Panikerum* 17, 88–89, 227
Satchidanandan, Anand, K. 1–3,
    88, 91–93, 117, 181, 205
    Kozhipanku 3
Satire 77, 158, 162, 196, 212
Screenplay 14–15, 53, 88, 102, 193
Selected Poems of Ayyappa Paniker
    xi–ii, 42, 61, 93, 101, 125, 165,
    211, 218, 230
Self-confidence 58, 83, 147, 171, 224
Self-Curse 219
Self-mockery 77, 158, 188
Sensibility xii, 12, 17–18, 32, 66
    literary 12, 18
    shift in 17
Sethumadhavan, A. (Sethu) 1, 122
    Ezham Pakkam 122
    Kaimudrakal 122
    Marupiravi 122
    Niyogam 13, 122
    Pandavapuram 122

Thingalaazhchakalile Aakaasham 122
Shashtipoorthi celebrations 26–27
Shatrubhayam 61
Shatrumithram 62, 203
Sheriyum Thettum 203
Short story(ies) 3, 21, 122, 138, 143, 207
South and North 62, 197–98, 203
Sreekantan Nair, C.N. 53, 65, 72, 141
   death anniversary 141
   Kanchana Sita 15, 53
   Lanka Lakshmi 53, 72, 141
   Saketam 53
Sreekumar, B. 206
   Ayyappa Paniker: Cholkkazhachayum Chollaakkazhachayum 206
Sree Narayana Guru 150, 164, 214
Sreenath Nair, Dr 43–44
   Devashilakal 43
Study Centre for Indian Literature in English and Translation (SCILET) 186
Sugathakumari 2–3, 76, 117, 157
   Krishna nee enne ariyilla ... 76, 157
   Rathrimazha 3

Teacher–student relationship 34
Thampan, Dr M.R. 31–32, 192
Theatre 29, 53, 64–66, 73
   indigenous 65, 66
The Island 197
The Peacock and the Moonlight 199
The Stone 228
The Three Pioneers of Malayalam Cinema 66
The Wheel 102, 200–201
Thilahomam 221
Translations xvii, 16, 42, 53–55, 90, 93, 106, 113, 125, 137–38, 140, 142–43, 174, 181–82

Udayaasthamanam 203
Ulysses 128, 129
Union Christian (UC) College, Aluva xvii, 1, 3–4, 13–14
University College, Thiruvananthapuram 13, 28, 54, 72, 93, 140, 153
University of Kerala, Thiruvananthapuram xvii, 5, 14–15, 18, 26, 34, 59, 115, 153, 192
Unniraja, C. 160, 180, 206, 228
US 8, 58, 108, 110, 122, 182, 187, 223

Vayalar Award 41
Vella Meghangal 195
Venu, Nedumudi 65, 68–70, 77, 141
Vijayan, O.V. 1, 3, 143
Vinayachandran, D. 2, 24, 52
Vishwa Sahithyangaliloode 46, 82
Vyakti Chitrangal, Yatra Drishyangal 37, 125, 148, 159, 179–80, 228, 231

White Clouds 195
Whitman, Walt 8–9
   Passage to India 8
Without Waking Up 220
World Malayali 73, 107–08, 110
Writers
   contemporary 171
   modernist 3–4, 33
   young 36, 171

Young poets 27–28, 52–53, 89, 118, 129, 171

About the Author

PRIYADAS G. MANGALATH was a student of Dr Ayyappa Paniker at the Institute of English, University of Kerala. After earning a Master's degree in journalism, he served as a visiting faculty in the Department of Mass Communication and Journalism at Madras Christian College (MCC), Chennai. Priyadas collaborated with Salman Rushdie (1987–88) on a film for a television series based on Rushdie's novel, *Midnight's Children*. He was the managing director of Guild Exports and Guild Soft Pvt. Ltd, Thiruvananthapuram, and the editor of *Sankramanam*, a magazine published from Thiruvananthapuram. His publishing firm, also named Sankramanam, brought out books on modern Malayalam poetry, drama and films. He has also contributed critical articles to both English and Malayalam newspapers and magazines. His email id is priyadasg@gmail.com.

About the Translator

RADHIKA P. MENON, a Malayalam to English translator, taught English at Fatima Mata National College, Kollam, Kerala, for 25 years. Her notable translations include K. Madhavan's *On the Banks of the Tejaswini* (National Book Trust), Devaki Nilayangode's *Antharjanam* (Oxford University Press), S.K. Pottekkatt's *Tales of Athiranippadam* (Orient Black Swan), Moyarath Sankaran's *Autobiography* (Chinta), M.K. Sanoo's *Dr Palpu* (Open Door Media), Joseph Muliyil's *Sukumari* (Folio), Dr Sosamma Iype's *The Vechur Cow: A New Lease of Life* (Vechur Conservation Trust) and K.K. Kochu's *Dalithan* (Speaking Tiger).

In 2011, she was awarded the International Center for Writing and Translation (ICWT) Award by the University of California, Irvine, for her translation of *Tales of Athiranippadam*. She shared this honour with Sreedevi K. Nair, the professor who collaborated with her on the translation.